FEARLESS FREDDIE

FEARLESS FREDDIE

THE LIFE AND TIMES OF FREDDIE MILLS

CHRISTOPHER EVANS

First published by Pitch Publishing, 2017

Pitch Publishing
A2 Yeoman Gate
Yeoman Way
Worthing
Sussex
BN13 3QZ
www.pitchpublishing.co.uk
info@pitchpublishing.co.uk

A CIP catalogue record is available for this book
from the British Library.

ISBN 978-1-78531-282-3

Typesetting and origination by Pitch Publishing
Printed in the UK by TJ International, Cornwall

Contents

For Zachariah

Acknowledgements

Even though Freddie Mills had been dead a full decade before I was born, his story has always held a fascination for me. Perhaps it was my Great Auntie Joyce, born and bred in Bethnal Green, who first spiked my interest in him.

On one of her many visits to my grandmother's house in Ynyshir in the Rhondda, over a cup of tea she used to regale the family with stories of her life growing up in the East End. I can still remember her telling us 'I knew Ronnie and Reggie, they would do anything for anyone,' and then, tapping her nose with her index finger, she would give us a knowing look and say, 'I know who did Fred but I ain't saying.'

I once asked her who Fred was and she told me Freddie Mills was the most famous boxer in the land, a world champion who got in with some villains and they shot him dead. Over the years, I came to discover that my auntie's version of how Freddie met his demise was one of the tamer stories about his life.

No one in any walk of life has had their reputation tarnished as much as Freddie has since his death. Based on little or no evidence, he has been subject to a variety of scurrilous stories. In writing this book I hope to focus more on how he lived his life rather than how he died.

This book would never have happened without Paul and Jane Camillin of Pitch Publishing, who believed in this project from the start and have been an absolute pleasure to work with. I would also like to thank my editor, Mark Turley, whose patience especially when we were working on this book in the middle of a General Election campaign was limitless. I learned so much from Mark and am grateful for his help and advice.

I spent an enjoyable afternoon with retired referee and boxing historian, Wynford Jones, who shared his memories of his long boxing career and gave me some invaluable material about Freddie. Miles Templeton of boxinghistory.co.uk was an absolute mine of information, providing newspaper reports of Freddie's fights as well as being generous with his time when I was asking all sorts of questions. My thanks also to Nigel Baker of *Boxing Monthly* who was always on hand to point me in the right direction.

When writing about a boxer, the archive at *Boxing News* is a priceless resource and many of their reports gave a flavour of Freddie the boxer as did the website Boxrec. While researching this book I spent many hours at the National Archive in Kew; it is a fantastic facility and the staff there could not have been more helpful.

Thanks also to my mother who got me hooked on books from a young age and to Bob, my stepfather for putting up with all my Freddie anecdotes. Murphy, my faithful Labrador, must take some of the credit as it was our long walks in the Welsh valleys that provided the welcome distraction I needed to clear my head and plan out many of the chapters.

I could never have written this book without the support of my wife, Julia, who was heavily pregnant while I was researching Freddie's life and then looking after our beautiful baby son Zachariah while I was writing it.

Finally, I would like to thank Freddie Mills. I thoroughly enjoyed getting to know him by writing his story. I can only hope I have done him justice.

Introduction
This is your life

AFTER weeks of meticulous planning, everything was in place. The Irishman lay in wait and there was no way he was going to let his man get away. They were close friends but this was business. The target, former light-heavyweight champion of the world Freddie Mills, had no knowledge of what was about to happen to him.

The ex-boxer had been in the Irishman's sights for years. It would only be minutes before Freddie arrived. Silently, the Irishman watched as Freddie, oblivious to anything untoward, walked past without acknowledging him. Everything was going according to plan.

Earlier in the week, Freddie had received a phone call out of the blue. An old associate had a business proposition for him. It had the potential to make them both very wealthy but he had to keep it secret. Intrigued, Freddie agreed to meet. It was this premise which had brought him to this place.

Taking his opportunity, the Irishman emerged from the shadows. He was now only inches away from Freddie, close enough to tap him on the shoulder. Once the former boxer turned around, the Irishman looked him dead in the eye. He enjoyed watching people's faces as he completed his task. He never knew what the reaction would be. Most were surprised, some got angry but only a few had got away.

Usually Freddie would greet his old friend with a smile and hug, but not tonight. His first reaction was to ask what the Irishman was doing there. Then he noticed he was carrying something suspicious under his arm. Freddie knew instinctively he had been set up. At first, he was puzzled, then shocked when it finally dawned on him the purpose of the Irishman's mission.

All Freddie could do was give a resigned look as if to say, 'Ok, you finally got me,' before Eamonn Andrews, in his familiar Irish brogue, announced with a wide grin, 'Freddie Mills, tonight This is Your Life!'

'You're joking, is this on the level?' a stunned Freddie asked before the introduction music began and the studio curtains parted to begin another edition of the popular television show.

For an enjoyable half an hour, Freddie sat as family and friends shared anecdotes. His mother Lottie and brother Charlie recalled how he started boxing while growing up in Bournemouth. His first manager Jack Turner and former fighter Gypsy Daniels related stories of his days on the boxing booths. His wife Chrissie and daughter Susan said Freddie was the same in private as he was in public, full of fun, a real joker.

The man Freddie outpointed for the world championship in 1948, Gus Lesnevich, was flown in especially from New York City to playfully ask his former adversary for a rematch. Freddie reacted by laughing and calling his old foe 'one hell of a fighter'.

The final guest was one of the top comedians and entertainers of the day, Dickie Henderson, who told a few funny stories about how his mate Freddie, a regular in television, films and theatre, had a habit of letting his nerves get the better of him before a performance and kept forgetting his lines.

Before officially presenting the big red book at the end of the programme, Eamonn Andrews expressed the view that Freddie's ferocity in the ring, matched by his infectious personality, had secured him a place in the nation's hearts. As the audience clapped, Freddie, who had his youngest daughter in his arms, acknowledged their cheers as he had done throughout his ring career.

No one watching the happy scene at home at the beginning of 1961 could have imagined that, just over four years later, Freddie the family man would be found dead at the back of his nightclub, slumped in his car with a gunshot wound to his right eye after apparently blowing his own brains out.

Those who woke up to the news on 25 July 1965 were in shock. They could not believe the happy-go-lucky Mills would do something as awful as leave his wife widowed and their children without a father – least of all those who knew him best, his family.

They never accepted the verdict of the coroner, who ruled Freddie committed suicide in the grip of depression. To them, something sinister was afoot. Chrissie Mills ended her days convinced her husband had been murdered.

This speculation has not helped Freddie's reputation since his passing. Over the years, myths, rumours and salacious gossip about Freddie have been reported as fact. Of the raft of books and news articles which have been written about him, very few have focused on what he achieved in the ring.

In the 1940s, there was no bigger star in British boxing than Freddie and long before he fought for world championship he could confidently lay claim to another title – that of people's champion. His all-action style and non-stop punching saw him produce some of the most exciting fights seen in British boxing rings. Just having his name on a poster would almost certainly guarantee a sell-out. He was champion before the plethora of world titles that came later, when it meant he could rightfully call himself the best in the world.

He was also a showbusiness personality. At a time when sportsmen and women in Britain were seen and not heard outside arenas, Freddie was a familiar face in the early days of television, either presenting the pop show, *Six-Five Special*, or appearing as a guest star on various light entertainment shows. From time to time he would pop up in British films of the day, usually playing the tough guy. Others, like Henry Cooper and Frank Bruno, would follow the same path but Freddie got there first.

He was also an entrepreneur who used his ring and television earnings to become a successful businessman long after he retired. In the decade after his career ended, he ran one of the very first Chinese restaurants in London, enjoyed the proceeds of a buy-to-let property empire before turning his hand to running a nightclub. By the time tennis player David Lloyd had set up his successful leisure club chain or Manchester City's Francis Lee had launched his recycling business, Freddie had already been there and done it years before.

Above all, Mills was a trailblazer. It was during the darkness and gloom of the post-war years that he became a superstar, illuminating the lives of millions of Britons as they tried to piece together a country still coming to terms with the aftermath of the Second World War. In him they invested their hopes and dreams. This is his story.

1

A pair of roller skates

THE tall headmaster who held himself ramrod straight, giving a hint to the military man he once had been, cast his eye over the crowded classroom at St Michael's Primary School in Bournemouth. He knew exactly who he was looking for and his stern glare fixed itself on the boy at the back. Pointing his finger directly at the lad with a mop of dark, curly hair and cherubic features, Mr Bryan left none of the children in any doubt who he wanted to speak to.

'Mills! You boy, come with me. I want a word with you!' the headmaster yelled. The short, stocky lad obediently stood up and followed him out of the classroom. As they both left, the children, who had been frightened into silence by the presence of their headmaster, whispered to themselves, 'What has Freddie done this time?'

To the schoolchildren and those who lived near him, Freddie Mills had a reputation. It was not a good one. Other children knew better than to cross him. Do as he said or you ran the risk of being set upon after school. Young Freddie was not averse to using his fists to get his own way. Not that he used them much anyway. A threat usually did the trick.

The neighbours in Terrace Road, where Freddie was born and grew up, knew better than to leave anything valuable lying around. They used to say if it wasn't nailed down then Mills was bound to nick it. Anything which did come into his possession he usually sold to buy cigarettes.

As Freddie followed the headmaster, he had an inkling of what he wanted to speak to him about. The day before he had had a run-in with a copper, who asked him if he knew anything about a pair of stolen roller skates which the police officer held in his hands.

'I don't know nothing about any roller skates, never seen them before in my life,' said Freddie.

'Then why was I given your name by someone who was found with them?' Freddie shrugged his shoulders and walked away. He thought that was the end of it until Mr Bryan pointed to him in class that morning.

Once inside the headmaster's study, Freddie was met by the same policeman and another boy. 'This boy has given me your name. He says you sold him the roller skates after breaking into a derelict house.' Again Freddie lied. He and the other boy had indeed broken into the house. They found nothing except the roller skates. The first time he gave them a go, he fell flat on his face and grazed his arm. He then offloaded them to the other boy in the study.

Despite repeated warnings that he was in serious trouble, Freddie was steadfast in his refusal to admit anything. He hoped the copper would give in before he would. It did not work. He left school that morning with a note for his mother informing her he was summonsed along with his accomplice to appear before the magistrate court at 10am sharp the following day.

Ever since Freddie, the youngest of four children, was born on 19 June 1919, his mother Lottie and father Tom, a rag-and-bone man, had found life tough. Money was tight and the last thing they needed was to pay a court fine should their son be found guilty.

'Oh, Freddie what is to become of you?' his mother despaired. Even though Bournemouth was seen as a desirable place to live for the affluent, it still had a dark underbelly. There were very few opportunities for working class boys anyway, let alone someone who had acquired a criminal record before he reached working age.

A constant reminder of the harshness of life was a mission found at the bottom of their street, where a hot meal or bed for the night was offered to anyone who had fallen on hard times. Both Tom and Lottie used to threaten Freddie that unless he pulled his socks up, he would end up there with the deadbeats and down-and-outs. Freddie would simply laugh. He was cocky enough to think he was too clever for that.

Despite being offered several opportunities to confess, the two boys who stood in the dock remained silent. Freddie believed he would win the battle of wills with the judge while his co-accused was too afraid of Freddie, and the retribution he might mete out, to say anything which would incriminate them both.

It was midday before the magistrate grew tired of the boys' act. Splitting them up, Freddie was taken to another room away from his friend, who remained in the court. Upon his return, he was told the other boy had burst into tears, admitted everything and said he had been bullied into it. Left with no choice, Freddie confessed, was fined a pound and placed on probation for two years.

Apart from having to pay a fine the family could ill afford, Freddie was met with more shame that night as his father Tom had left the evening paper open on the kitchen table. The page told all of Bournemouth that his son had appeared in court that day and confessed to burglary and handling stolen goods. Now it was official. Freddie was a thief.

After Freddie went to bed that night, Tom and Lottie talked about their son's future. 'The boy needs discipline. He will have to learn to box. What was good for our Charlie will be good for our Freddie,' they decided.

Boxing ran in the family. Freddie's brother Charlie was a useful boxer who had earned extra money on the boxing booths and held a four-fight professional record. Having grown increasingly worried by Freddie's wild ways, Lottie reached the end of her tether with her youngest son and reluctantly agreed to allow Tom and Charlie to teach Freddie to box. The day after his court appearance, Freddie laced on a pair of Charlie's old scuffed, oversized gloves in the back yard. Taking on his older brother with his father acting as referee, Freddie imagined he was Jack 'Kid' Berg, the Whitechapel Windmill, and tore into Charlie, but found only thin air.

With his father shouting encouragement, Freddie tried and tried to land a punch on his sibling but failed. After a few minutes chasing without much luck, an exhausted Freddie collapsed on the floor gasping for breath.

Rather than being despondent, Freddie was fascinated by how Charlie had managed to evade his best punches. Besides, he did not like being made a fool of. He was determined to master this boxing game. Holding up the palms of his hands and inviting Freddie to punch, Charlie taught his brother how to stand properly, throw a jab and land an uppercut.

His training continued at the local youth club. With no other boys to spar with, Freddie would regularly share the ring with a man with a wooden leg, who showed him how to sidestep an attack and move his head to avoid an incoming punch. Immediately, Freddie fell in love with boxing. Each week, he was always the first to arrive and the last to leave.

By the time his 11th birthday came around, there was only one thing on Freddie's wish list – a pair of boxing gloves. Despite meeting with resistance from his mother, who had recently witnessed a beating her elder son suffered in the boxing booths, he received his very own pair.

Underneath the street lamp, Freddie and his friends would re-enact all the famous fights of the day. One day he would pretend to be Jack Dempsey while another boy would play Gene Tunney. With no ring, these bouts would go on late into the night, starting at one end of the street only to finish at the other.

Lying in bed at night, all Freddie thought about was boxing. He dreamt of headlining the Winter Gardens in Bournemouth for the world heavyweight title. He closed his eyes and visualised knocking out Len Harvey, who had just become British middleweight champion, or facing off against Harvey's great rival Jock McAvoy.

Every waking hour was consumed by boxing. Even when doing the odd jobs he carried out to earn some extra money, Freddie always had boxing in mind.

Carrying potato sacks for the local greengrocers in the early morning strengthened his shoulders. Riding out on a bicycle to the countryside and digging for worms, which he sold to fishermen, developed his legs. Even when he helped his brother-in-law on his milk round, he would carry his boxing gloves in the hope of impromptu bouts with some of the boys.

The physical training was not the only reason Freddie took on these jobs. He had not grown up in the Mills household without knowing there was little money to go around. Lottie was a housewife and the nature of Tom's business meant there were days when it was a struggle to put food on the table.

Paying Freddie's fine meant the family would have to go without for a few weeks. Ever since that day in court, Freddie had been consumed with guilt. He had to pay his mother back.

The proudest moment of Freddie's young life came one night over the dinner table. Handing over a crisp pound note to his mother, Freddie beamed, 'Here you go mum, here's that pound I owe you for my fine. Don't worry, I've been saving my money from my odd jobs for it.'

Moved to tears, Lottie looked at her youngest son. Perhaps he really was turning a corner at long last. His father winked and nodded. Freddie had done the right thing.

The proceeds from these business ventures gave Freddie some ready money. Some of it was put towards buying clothes while most went on converting the garden shed into a homemade gymnasium, complete with a punch bag and speed ball. It was not long before the back yard coaching sessions, on Sundays after church, with Charlie and Tom became full-blooded fights, with Lottie having to sew and mend ripped shirts and trousers, such was the ferocity between the brothers.

Despite the new-found discipline which boxing brought to Freddie's life, he still managed to get into scrapes. One such incident would inadvertently set him on a career path that would see him go from facing off against his brother, with his father as the only spectator, to being cheered by thousands in some of the biggest sporting arenas in the country.

2

Climbing a ladder

NERVOUSLY, Freddie walked up to the front door of promoter Jack Turner. It had been a week since he noticed the poster asking for novice boxers to enter a tournament to be held at the Westover Ice Rink in Bournemouth.

Several times Freddie had been up the street where the promoter lived, only to turn around before even getting to his door.

After the initial euphoria of seeing the poster, doubts about his ability plagued him. Even though he had been boxing for five years, his experience was limited to street fights and his weekly sessions at the youth club.

'What's the matter with you? This is your big chance. What are you waiting for?' asked Percy Cook, the milkman, whom Freddie had been apprenticed to when he left school a year earlier. He was also the brother of Welsh lightweight champion Gordon.

'I just don't know, it's a big step up,' responded Freddie.

Percy could not believe his ears. Ever since he was teamed up with the youngster, it was boxing morning, noon and night. Freddie idolised Gordon Cook and wanted to know everything about him. How he got started, what food he ate and how many rounds he sparred in training.

When Freddie was not talking about boxing, he was taking part in impromptu bouts Percy arranged between the apprentices, which took place in the hour between two morning rounds.

Just watching Freddie dominate the other boys, Percy knew he was witnessing a special talent. When he stepped in the ring to spar, he was impressed with his rapid head movement and clever sidestep. The more he saw Freddie in action, the more he was convinced he would go far in the boxing world.

'Go on Freddie, I'll drop you off, Jack's a good man. He'll look after you. Get in with him and the world's your oyster,' Percy told a visibly nervous Freddie as he dropped him off outside Turner's house, promising to wait for him until after he had spoken to the promoter.

After a few deep breaths, Freddie overcame his nerves and gingerly knocked on the door. Within seconds, Jack Turner answered. Freddie took one look at him and thought, 'Shit!'

It was not the first time Freddie had come face-to-face with the promoter. One Friday, Jack Turner presented a boxing bill at Bournemouth Winter Gardens and local fighter Jack Lewis was the headline. Locally, he had a bit of a following and Freddie was determined to see him. The only problem was after paying his mother board and lodge, he did not have enough money to pay the entrance fee.

However, Freddie would not be foiled. After scouring around for a discarded ticket which he hoped he could use to gain entry, he saw a disused ladder.

With a friend, he hauled it against the building and clambered on to the roof, which had a glass dome shaped like a gherkin. After climbing across, they found a window they could open, undoing the latch. They could see Jack Lewis, who looked about two foot tall from their vantage point, facing off in the main event.

Every Friday, Jack Turner would put on a show and for the rest of the month the boys would follow the same routine. Wind or rain, it did not matter as long as Freddie could watch some boxing, such was his obsession with the sport. The enterprise came to an abrupt halt when Jack Turner caught the boys halfway up the ladder and chased them off.

When the young man knocked on his door, Turner had long forgotten about the incident and had no idea who Freddie was. 'Yes, can I help you?'

'I'm ... I'm ... Freddie Mills and I want to enter the boxing tournament,' Freddie stammered.

Turner smiled and invited the young boxer in. Within minutes, Freddie was telling the promoter about his brother Charlie, Percy and Gordon Cook. To Jack Turner, it was quite clear he had a boxing nut on his hands.

'I think you are just what we are looking for. Bring your kit to the ice rink next Friday,' he said.

Fight night arrived and Freddie was at the ice rink early. He was anxious but keen to make a good impression. The dressing room was full of seasoned professionals. Some were quietly loosening up while others had their hands wrapped. Freddie, who had never even been inside a boxing arena let alone a ring before, sat feeling every inch the rookie.

'It's Freddie Mills, isn't it? My brother tells me good things about you. He's asked me to work your corner tonight.' Freddie looked up. He could not believe his idol Gordon Cook was standing before him, offering to help him out.

After walking to the ring with only a towel around his shoulders, Gordon gave Freddie just one piece of advice. 'Enjoy it, relax and remember everything you have learned.'

Both novices were apprehensive as they sized one another up. It was Freddie who attacked first, launching himself at the other boy with a flurry of punches to head and body. It was clear the other boy had no interest in exchanging with Freddie and a swift left hook to the head ended matters after only 30 seconds of round one.

The boy was counted out but Freddie stood there dumbfounded, rooted to the spot. 'You've won!' shouted Gordon Cook. Still Freddie did not move. It was not until the referee told him to get out of the ring that his victory began to sink in.

After the bout, Jack Turner told Freddie to return the following week for the next round of the tournament. The final would take place a fortnight later.

'Here you are, mum, a lovely rose bowl for the mantelpiece.'

Fearing Freddie had reverted back to his old ways, Lottie asked her youngest son where he had got it from.

'I won it boxing,' answered Freddie. He then told his mother how over the past three weeks he had been boxing every Friday night in a tournament, where he had knocked out three boys. His longest fight was the final, which had taken him three rounds to win.

No one was more shocked than Freddie when he won. After knocking out his opponent, Young Barfoot, he was about to leave the ring for the dressing room when Gordon Cook pulled him back.

'Stay here, you've won!' Gordon said.

'Well yes,' said Freddie. 'When do I turn up again?'

'You don't,' Gordon answered. 'You've won the final. Stop in the ring, they're going to give you a prize.'

Minutes later, standing in the ring, Freddie posed for a photograph holding the rose bowl. His picture would appear in the morning paper, where he was billed as 'a star of the future.'

After reading the article, his deadpan father said to his disapproving mother, 'Well Lottie, it beats being called a thief!'

Later that night, Freddie carefully cut out the story in the paper and pasted it into a scrapbook. He would meticulously record every newspaper article for the rest of his career.

The aftermath of the competition was an anti-climax for Freddie. There were no more fights on the horizon and training seemed futile. He was doing well at the dairy. However, Freddie was bored. The tournament had only whetted his appetite. He wanted to be like his mentor Gordon Cook, a professional boxer.

Smashing his fists into the punch bag in his shed, Freddie's concentration was broken by the sound of his father calling out to him. 'Freddie, Freddie can you come in here, please?' Freddie was annoyed. If there was one thing he hated more than anything, it was being called away from his training.

'Ok, Dad, be there in a minute.'

'Can you come now?' was his father's response. Fearing the worst, Freddie pulled off his boxing gloves and walked into the house. Sitting there, waiting in the lounge, was Jack Turner. Tom spoke first, telling Freddie the promoter had a very interesting proposition for him.

Like the Cook brothers, Jack Turner had been hugely impressed by Freddie's performances in the boxing tournament. He had potential. Sitting there in the lounge with his father, Jack smiled at Freddie.

'Well, young Mills, how would you like another fight? There is a fighter called George Hasket. I think you pair would be well matched. The fight will take place in three weeks' time. You can train with my brother Bob at the local gym we use and what's more you'll get paid. How does that sound?'

All Freddie's dreams were coming true. Jack Turner was offering to make him a professional fighter. Trying to stop himself from getting carried away, Freddie asked his father what he thought. Tom told him it was his decision. There was no hesitation. He replied by asking when he got started.

The Lower Parkstone Gymnasium was worlds away from the garden shed and youth club Freddie was used to. The place hung heavy with the sweat of hard work as boxers jumped rope, shadow boxed in full-length mirrors and worked the speed ball.

Within minutes of meeting Jack's brother Bob, Freddie was stripped to the waist, wearing 16oz boxing gloves and facing off against another boxer on the bill in Weymouth, Harry Conquest.

After a fortnight of hard training, Freddie was ready. Travelling down with Harry and Bob to the Alexandra Gardens Theatre, Weymouth, he tried to block out all the nerves he was feeling. This was his opportunity and he was not going to waste it. He was going to repay the faith Jack Turner had shown in him.

Sat in the dressing room waiting to be called, Freddie repeatedly hit his fist into his glove. He had only one thing on his mind and that was beating George Haskett. Even when his training partner returned from his own bout with a split lip and broken nose, Freddie took little notice and was determined not to lose his focus.

Wearing a new gumshield and boxing trunks, he was finally in the ring with the man who had dominated his thoughts over the past few weeks, George Haskett. In his mind, he was much bigger and more menacing than he was in the flesh.

Waiting for the bell to sound, the only time Freddie took his eyes off his opponent was when he saw his friend's blood on the canvas from the previous fight. Once the bell rang he was like an animal unleashed, tearing into Haskett.

The more seasoned Weymouth man used lateral movement and his jab to keep Freddie at bay. Despite Freddie getting a few heavy shots in, most who watched the bout were in agreement with the referee's decision to award a draw. For his trouble, Mills was paid a grand total of 18s and 6d, or 92 and half pence in new money.

Over a celebratory meal of fish and chips, Bob Turner offered to be Freddie's manager, a role he was to serve for the next five years, taking 25 per cent of his earnings.

Days later, they registered a contract with the British Boxing Board of Control. Freddie Mills could finally claim to be a professional boxer. He had taken his first steps on the road to boxing stardom but there would be many twists and turns along the way before he got there.

3

Following the fair

AFTER wandering around the stalls and sideshows of the fairground for over half an hour, Freddie was lost. He had been told to catch the train to Exeter, where he would be met by either Jack or Bob Turner, but when he arrived they were nowhere to be seen.

Not wanting to hang around at the train station any longer than he needed to, Freddie hitched a ride down to the local show field, where the fair was just being set up. He was sure he would bump into one of the brothers there sooner or later.

Thinking it was all a waste of time, Freddie wondered whether to turn around and go home to Bournemouth. It was then he spied a large, tanned man tightening up the guide ropes on a boxing booth. 'Excuse me, I'm looking for Bob Turner or his brother Jack. My name's Freddie Mills and I'm here to join the boxing booths.'

The boxing booth had been a feature of British fairs since the 18th century. Fighters signed up for a few months and travelled with the booth from town to town. They were given food and lodgings and paid a small wage for their services. Their real money was made through 'nobbins', coins thrown into the ring by spectators as a show of appreciation after they had fought.

The man smiled at him. 'So you're Freddie, then? Jack's told me all about you,' he said. Extending his hand, the man introduced himself as, 'Daniels, Bill Daniels, but I fight under the name of Gypsy Daniels.'

'Well, son, you got your clobber? Jack told me to help show you the digs.'

Upon hearing the name, Freddie was taken aback. Gypsy Daniels had taken on almost mythic status. A Welshman who had travelled to New York City, where he eventually took on and beat the former world heavyweight champion Max Schmeling, Gypsy was now offering to help Freddie get settled into his new surroundings.

Just a week earlier, Freddie had taken the momentous decision to pack in his job at the dairy and pursue a life on the fair grounds. Even though Freddie was undefeated throughout the past 18 months, the Turner brothers worried he was not developing quickly enough. Most of his wins were coming via early knockouts, which were not giving him a chance to develop his boxing skills.

A bout against Jim McKnight, a contender for the middleweight crown of Ireland, was seen as a step up in class for Freddie and started the alarm bells ringing. For the first eight rounds, McKnight allowed Freddie to load up haymakers only for them to pass harmlessly over his head, as he used his ring craft to avoid Mills' more dangerous punches.

After chasing the Irishman for nine rounds, Freddie finally caught up with the rapidly tiring McKnight. In the last three rounds, Freddie put on a devastating display of body punching, picking up a hard-fought win from the referee.

Afterwards, Jack and Bob weren't happy. It was only Freddie's superior fitness that had got him through the fight. Both agreed for their man to develop he had to get more rounds under his belt. As luck would have it, Jack had been given the option of running the boxing marquee at Chipperfield's Circus. It was the ideal place for Freddie to learn his trade.

By joining the booth, Freddie was following the well-worn path trodden by such fighters as Rhondda natives Jimmy Wilde and Tommy Farr. It was a hard life but gave unrivalled experience to a young fighter in a short space of time.

The following day, the Turner brothers were at Freddie's house. He had a good idea why they were there. In the lounge, Freddie sat down and listened to what the brothers had to say.

'Look here, Fred, you're doing quite nicely as a part-time boxer but how about making it your career?'

'Just a minute,' Freddie answered, standing up to close the living room door so his suspicious mother wouldn't overhear the conversation. 'Well, if you think I am good enough, what do you have in mind?'

'Both of us think you are good enough,' Jack replied with a smile. 'Play your cards right and you could have a big future in the fight game.'

Jack continued, 'You will not get far if you stay in the dairy much longer. Now if you agree, my idea is to take you travelling on the boxing booths around the West Country. What do you think?'

It would mean leaving home and fighting all-comers up to eight times a day, but the experience would be invaluable. Freddie was excited by the idea and wanted to say yes on the spot, but first he had to talk his sceptical mother around. Dealing with Lottie was no mean feat but knowing how much

Freddie loved boxing and how bored he was of the dairy, she reluctantly gave him her blessing.

By the end of the week, dressed in a brand new Marks and Spencer's navy suit and carrying a brown leather attaché case, Freddie was on the train heading to his new life.

After meeting his landlady at his new home, the Alexandra Inn, Freddie unpacked and washed before Jack Turner finally arrived. 'Sorry, Freddie, had a bit of business to attend to. The circus has only just arrived in town, so things are a little slow. You will have to go in the crowd and gee.'

Freddie did not have a clue what Jack was talking about. 'Gee?'

Jack explained that at regular shows the booth could not always rely on getting somebody from the crowd who was willing to go either three or even six rounds. So there was always one or more of the regular fighters in the crowd. If there was no one forthcoming, the 'gee' would call out and accept the challenge as though they were there for the fun of it.

Disappointed not to be fighting, Freddie put his blue suit on again and went back to the fair ground with Bob Turner, who was going to tell him what to do.

No one in the crowd would have guessed Freddie's true identity as he stood amongst them waiting for the sound of the trumpet, which told the audience the boxing show was about to begin. Freddie looked up as Jack Turner began, 'Ladies and gentlemen. Who in the crowd is tough enough to take on the Romany King, Mr Gypsy Daniels?'

Standing on a platform in front of a lavishly painted portico, depicting ring heroes of yesteryear, stripped to the waist, was the man who had introduced himself earlier in the day as Bill Daniels. He was wearing a bright red bandana with what looked like an old curtain hook hanging from his ear. The smiling, friendly giant was gone. Gypsy Daniels was now fully in character.

'There is no man alive who can last more than three rounds with me!' he said.

Dangling a pair of well-worn gloves, Jack challenged the crowd. There were no takers.

After a few more minutes, Bob shouted out, 'Hey mate, I got the man, Fred Mills is his name, and he's standing here. We call him the Knockout Kid back home in Bournemouth. He'll take Daniels on.'

'Well, well, we have heard all about young Mr Mills. He's hot stuff. What do you reckon, Gypsy? Do you accept the challenge?' Jack asked the man on the platform.

'Accept? I will eat him alive!'

Very soon, Freddie had stripped off his shirt, jacket and tie. Sat on the stool in the ring that Daniels had erected earlier in the day, Bob Turner laced on Freddie's gloves. 'Don't worry, Freddie, Bill knows it's your first go. Just follow his lead.'

Any hopes Daniels was going to take it easy on Freddie disappeared after the opening bell. Within seconds, the man who had held his own in the tough gymnasiums of Brooklyn smashed Freddie clean on the jaw with a powerful right hook. He followed this up with a straight left that brought blood to Freddie's nostrils.

Once they got into a clinch Daniels, who outweighed Freddie by four stone, pushed down on his opponent's shoulders. When Jack Turner, who was acting as referee, tried to break the fighters up, Daniels held Freddie in a headlock, shouting to the crowd it was all too easy for him.

As the round ended and Freddie returned to his stool, Daniels walked around the ring with his hands held triumphantly in the air, drawing loud boos from the crowd.

When the bell rang for the second, Freddie tried mixing it with Daniels, which got the crowd on his side. All Freddie's good work was undone when Daniels deliberately hit Freddie blow the belt, bringing the young fighter to his knees. As Jack Turner warned Daniels about his dirty tactics, Gypsy pleaded innocence.

Even trying to smother Daniels' best work did not help Freddie's cause as the older man had taken to punching on the break. Despite repeated warnings from Jack, Daniels received no sanctions for his constant fouling.

Before the bell began for the third, Jack came over to Freddie's corner and told him he was doing a great job. The crowd were reacting how they planned. Daniels was playing the villain. There were bound to be one or two boys in the audience who would enter the ring to challenge him after Freddie in an attempt to bring the cocksure Daniels down a peg or two.

In the third and final round, Daniels came up with a new tactic. Every time they got in close, he would blatantly headbutt Freddie. By now, the combination of punches combined with the impact of Daniels' skull was making Freddie feel dizzy and sick.

No one was more grateful when they heard the final bell than Mills. 'Ladies and gentlemen,' Jack Turner boomed on the mike. 'As is the custom, the boxers Daniels and Mills from the last fight, who put up such a good show, are now taking their hats round and I hope you will show your appreciation in the usual way. I thank you, ladies and gentlemen.'

Tonight had been a very good night. Both fighters shared £3 between them. Afterwards, Freddie collected his things and was given the night off. His brand new suit trousers were caked in blood, his head pounded and his ear had swollen to twice its size. Back at his digs he had little sleep, having spent most of the night throwing up.

After the last bout of the evening, Bob Turner turned to Gypsy Daniels and asked him what he thought of Freddie. 'He's a real tough kid, he took a lot of punishment but didn't moan once. I think he'll do all right.'

For Freddie, the first day on the booth had served as a harsh lesson in just how tough this way of life could be, but it did not deter him and he was back for more the following morning.

4

Special treatment

IT was cold and wet, it was the end of the summer and it had been impossible to sleep. The booth had pitched up at Devizes and there had been torrential rain for two weeks. The appalling weather had stopped people from coming to the booths. With no punters paying entrance money, fighters went unpaid. Increasingly, Freddie was getting fed up. Things had finally come to a head.

A military camp had been set up nearby and Bob Turner had been unable to secure digs for the boxers. The only place to bed down for the night was underneath a lorry, with an overcoat for a blanket. One night, a steady stream of rain forced Freddie into one of the trucks, which transported the booth from place to place. The roof from the cab leaked and all he could do was huddle there until morning.

The ground was sodden, so it was impossible to even set up the booth. Freddie seethed. Ever since the Turner brothers had left Chipperfield's for the McKeowen Family Boxing Booth, there had been problems. Freddie did not like the owner, Sam.

To make matters worse, Freddie complained to Bob Turner that he found the McKeowens unprofessional. Many of their pitches were unsuitable and they seemed plagued by travellers, who were more interested in bare knuckle fighting than the noble art of boxing.

To Sam McKeowen, who ran the booth with his wife Esther, Freddie was a lazy, cocky young upstart. He felt that Bob Turner was too easy on Freddie, giving him special treatment. When the other boys set up the booth, Bob excused Freddie, claiming he needed extra training and would run the risk of injury should he pull a muscle while pulling on the guide ropes.

A few times Freddie had gone missing from the booth, especially when they pitched up near the coast. One day, Sam found Freddie sunbathing on the beaches in Paignton. When he asked the young boxer what he was doing, Freddie said he had a fight coming up and Bob had told him he could have the afternoon off.

A few weeks later, Freddie was knocked out by George Davis from Notting Hill at a bout in Poole. Freddie had looked out of shape and was never in the fight against the future Southern Area middleweight champion. Mills blamed the haphazard way Sam ran his booths and Sam saw the loss as an example of Freddie being bone idle.

When Sam took the issue up with Bob Turner, the manager simply shrugged his shoulders and told the booth owner that Freddie had developed a following and was good for business. It did not help matters that Freddie had managed to charm Sam's wife, who everyone called Ma. A cheeky smile and a wink from Freddie and he could get away with murder with Mrs McKeowen.

It wasn't long before the other lads on the booth clocked the way Freddie was acting. Why was Freddie so special? It wouldn't be too long before things came to a head between Sam and Freddie.

Since moving booths, Freddie felt isolated. He really didn't get on with the other boys on the booth, who viewed him with suspicion. During his time with Chipperfield's, Freddie had developed a close friendship with Gypsy Daniels. They shared a room together whenever they travelled and the older man had become something of a mentor to him.

Daniels, who thought Freddie was one of the most talented boxers he had ever seen, had elected to stay with Chipperfield's. He told Freddie that joining the McKeowens was a mistake. He said the McKeowen family were small time and would do nothing for his development as a boxer. Feeling he owed the Turner brothers something, Freddie decided to follow them. Now, shivering cold in the early morning, he knew he had made a mistake. He missed Daniels and wanted out.

Climbing out of the cab, his clothes sodden wet, he encountered Sam McKeowen. 'You think this is fucking funny? I've had enough, Sam, I'm off home.'

Months of frustration boiled over. 'You can go fuck off and stay there,' Sam yelled back. 'If you get there, you'll find your cards waiting in the post for you.'

'Like I care! Fuck off, Sam!' Freddie shouted back, walking back with his gear in his now battered attaché case. Finally, after hitchhiking all the way back to Hampshire, he knocked on the front door of Terrace Road and a surprised Lottie answered the door. 'What are you doing here?' she asked.

A cold and wet Freddie embraced his mother. After a fortnight of sleeping rough, he was pleased to be back in the warmth of his mother's house. 'I've had it mum. You wouldn't believe the way we're treated. They couldn't even get us a bed for the night.'

'Freddie, I've told you, boxing's okay for a bit of fun but you'll never make a living out of it,' Lottie told her son.

'What am I going to do instead?' Freddie asked. 'Go back to the dairy?'

Telling her son he needed to learn a trade, it just so happened there was an opening at the local garage where Freddie could train to be a mechanic.

After being forced to pay a visit to the local garage owner, the following day Freddie began work at Westover Garage, which overlooked the ice rink.

On that first day, Freddie reported for work hardly dressed and ready to start work as a trainee mechanic, wearing the same smart blue suit he wore on his first day on the booths just two years earlier. By the Tuesday, the pristine new suit looked like an oily rag. Each night Freddie, who always took pride in his appearance, would scrub his hands in an effort to wash off the grime.

The garage overlooked the Westover Ice Rink, the site of many of Freddie's early-career triumphs. It proved too much of a distraction. Amidst the heat and grime of the garage, his mind would wander to thoughts of boxing matches and his care-free days on the booths. The pay of 50 shillings a week was not enough. He missed the opportunity to earn extra with the nobbins.

At the end of his second week, the manager turned to Freddie and said, 'It isn't working, is it?' He had just jacked up a car under a petrol tank and ruined it. The day before, while tightening up a wheel, he had managed to wrench a few nuts off.

Freddie agreed after a friendly handshake and his brief career in the motor trade came to an end.

After explaining what had happened to his mother, Lottie asked Freddie what he was going to do next. 'I need to fight, mum, it's the only thing I can do,' replied Freddie.

Getting back into the ring was harder than Freddie expected. He paid a visited to Bob Turner's house where his wife said the last time she had heard from him, both Turner brothers were leaving Brixham, Devon after a regatta there. That was a week ago and she had heard nothing since.

Thinking he had messed up his chances of ever boxing again, Freddie decided to help his father out on his round. Each morning, Freddie would wake up at 5am to get the horse ready for the day ahead. As autumn approached, Freddie got more and more depressed. He was back to where he started, resigned to working with his father for the rest of his life. Then his luck changed.

After a hard day, Freddie settled in front of the fire to read the paper. He turned to the situations vacant pages and noticed a small advertisement. It said the McKeowen family were planning to put on an evening of boxing that weekend in Weymouth. They challenged any local man to come along and test their skills against their champions.

It was just like the first time. Freddie had joined the booth as he arrived in Weymouth looking to make amends with Bob Turner. Finally, among the trapeze artists and freak shows, Freddie found Bob.

'Hello, Bob.' Freddie smiled at his manager as if nothing had happened. 'Freddie! Where've you been hiding? You've been missed,' replied Bob.

They walked together over to the boxing booth, which was built and ready for action. There, they met with Sam McKeowen. 'I have a good mind to knock your heads together,' said Bob. 'We could make each other serious money here. Now come on, shake hands.' Both Freddie and Sam reluctantly shook each other's hands. It was an uneasy truce.

It was like Freddie had never been away that night on the booths. Once back at his digs, Bob waited for him with a proposition. His brother Jack, who still promoted local favourite Jack Lewis, wanted to match two of Bournemouth's favourite fighters in December. It would mean a step up in class as Lewis was the reigning Western Area welterweight champion. If Freddie was interested, they could get the ball rolling straight away.

It took seconds for Freddie to reply. He could not believe it. Growing up, Lewis had been something of a local celebrity. It was the desire to watch Lewis fight that had driven Freddie up the roof of Bournemouth Winter Gardens just a few years earlier. Now he would be doing battle with him at the Westover Ice Rink. There, he was thinking just days before that his boxing career was at an end.

First, there was a warm-up fight earlier in the month, against Fred Clements. Demonstrating the type of aggressiveness Freddie had become renowned for, he gave Clements all he could handle. Knowing Jack Lewis was also appearing on the bill at the Westover Ice Rink, Freddie was determined to give him something to think about ahead of their fight in a couple of weeks' time.

Any hopes of an early knockdown were frustrated as Freddie chased the more defensive Clements around the ring. The fight sparked into life in the fifth round when Clements finally engaged with Mills. Any hopes of an exciting, drawn-out, full-blooded fight, which the bout had threatened to be in the previous round, were dashed when Clements' corner retired him with a suspected broken hand before the bell rang to start the sixth. It was a disappointing, hollow victory for Freddie.

Throughout training for the Lewis fight, after seeing Freddie become exasperated as he chased the more defensive Clements around the ring, Turner implored Freddie to slow down and pick his punches. Having been on the boxing scene for a long time, Lewis was a veteran, who would summon all his years of experience to keep Freddie at bay.

The new training headquarters above a garage in central Bournemouth were basic but much better than Freddie had enjoyed on the boxing booth. However, it still wasn't perfect. There was a single pane of glass in six window frames, allowing the bitter December air come in. A heavy bag and speed ball had been set up but some days it was too cold for Bob Turner to rub down Freddie and he had to do it at home instead.

Counting down the days to the fight, Freddie felt a mixture of excitement and nerves. He knew he would be fighting before a sell-out audience. He was determined to do well in front of his home town crowd. He had always enjoyed testing himself in the ring and on the boxing booths he relished taking on bigger men. In his mind, there was only one way to improve and that was to fight the best.

As Freddie made his way to the ring, he heard a familiar voice. 'Go on, Freddie, you can do this son!' It was Gordon Cook, who had come along to cheer his protégé on. Soon, he was face to face with Jack Lewis. After receiving his instructions from the referee, Bob Turner told Freddie, 'Remember, just take your time, and pick your moment.'

As expected, the fight had been a sell-out, with locals queuing for hours before the box office opened. The bell rang for the first round and the crowd were evenly split with cries of 'Mills, Mills, Mills' met with the shout of 'Llllleeeeewwwiss.' Freddie tried to drown out the shouts. He wanted to get down to business.

Both fighters circled each other. Remembering what Bob told him, Freddie waited for the first opportunity. He opened by launching a crunching right that landed on the forearms of Lewis, who had cupped his hands around his head in anticipation of the power punch. A left hook got through Lewis' guard but did not seem to unduly worry him for very long.

The early rounds saw Freddie on the front foot, impressing onlookers by picking his punches, leading some to believe he was enjoying a slight lead over Lewis, who adopted the tactics of defensively pushing out his left jab to keep Freddie at bay. When that didn't work, the more experienced Lewis resorted to holding, leading to a warning from the referee for grabbing Mills around the neck.

The crowd had expected to see fireworks between the two local fighters and got restless. Every time Mills attacked, Lewis fell into a clinch. After six rounds, there were calls from the crowd for Lewis to get stuck in.

Jack Lewis came out for the seventh looking like a different fighter. Adopting a much more aggressive style, he began to take the fight to Freddie, scoring effectively with rights about the head. A flashing right uppercut from Mills in the eighth shook Lewis but he quickly recovered to mete out more punishment. From that point, it was a clear Freddie was beginning to tire and every attack he launched began to peter out.

The last minute of the 10th round was the most thrilling of the fight. Despite looking out on his feet in the early parts of the round, mustering all the energy he could find, Freddie launched a two-fisted attack that rocked the more experienced Lewis. It was all in vain. The referee raised Lewis' hand in victory at the sound of the final bell. 'Hard luck, Freddie, he just had a bit more experience that's all,' Bob Turner told Freddie on his return to the corner.

Those watching were in agreement. Jack Lewis had just a bit too much ring craft for Freddie. All he needed was a couple more fights and the right training and he would have the beating of the likes of Lewis, Bob Turner told his brother Jack at the end of the bout. The more both Turner brothers watched their young fighter, the more they were convinced they had a future British champion on their hands.

5

On his terms

THE crowd at the Westover Ice Rink wanted blood. 'Cheat, cheat, cheat!' they shouted. An old woman sat in the front row and spat at Freddie. 'Mills, you dirty bastard,' she screamed. Just a few minutes earlier, the crowd had been cheering Freddie into the ring for a bout against Ted Barter. Now they were calling him all the names under the sun.

The Kingston fighter was another opponent Jack Turner had matched with Freddie as he built his man towards a rematch with Jack Lewis. The bout began with the usual belligerence from Mills, who pounded at the head and body of Barter. The crowd was firmly on the home town favourite's side.

By the fifth round, Freddie was well on top and left leads and right hooks saw Barter's face become a bloody mess. Watching from the corner, Bob Turner shouted from the corner for the referee to stop the fight. After pinning Barter in the corner, an overconfident Freddie rushed in for the kill but throwing caution to the wind he left himself wide open to a right cross from Barter.

The power of the punch caught Freddie by surprise. Losing his balance, he toppled over and landed hard on the floor.

Quickly using the ropes to haul himself to his feet before the referee could begin a count, an angry Freddie ran after Barter. Moving to the neutral corner, Barter turned his back on Freddie, who tapped him on the shoulder only to slam a hard right hook into his nose.

Now it was Barter's turn to visit the canvas. He landed with a thud before rolling out of the ring under the ropes. An irate Barter was back in the ring in no time throwing wild rights and lefts at Freddie. Some of these punches were more likely to be seen in a street fight than a boxing ring.

Thinking that Ted Barter had been hard done by, the crowd went wild. 'Chuck him out, referee!' someone shouted. The abuse continued as the bell rang to end the round. 'Don't listen to them, Freddie, you have done nothing wrong," Bob Turner reassured him. "Ted should've learnt the golden rule of boxing by now: protect yourself at all times.'

Things were made worse when the referee waved the fight off. Apparently, the unexpected right hook from Freddie had split Barter's nose in two. His corner could not stem the bleeding and it was affecting Barter's breathing. The bad feeling still lingered when Freddie went over to his opponent's corner. 'Fuck off, Mills, you bust his nose with that cheap shot. I hope you're pleased with yourself,' Barter's manager fumed.

An official complaint to disqualify Freddie for an illegal blow came to nothing. That did not stop the crowd pushing and jeering Mills as he left the ring for his dressing room. An ecstatic Jack Turner met up with Freddie a few days later. With his promoter's hat on, Jack thought things could not have turned out better in the Barter fight. To the Westover crowd, Freddie had become the bad guy.

So, the rematch with Jack Lewis was billed as the cocksure, young fighter, Freddie Mills, who would do anything to win, against the venerable old veteran, Jack Lewis, who always played by the rules. When they appeared on the bill just before their return, it was Freddie who was booed for the first time in his career as he dominated seaman Tommy Taylor, knocking him down several times in a lopsided decision over 12 rounds.

On the other hand, Jack Lewis was cheered to the rafters as he looked in magnificent form, knocking out Alf Tustain in three brutal rounds. Everything was set for a real needle match between the two Bournemouth fighters.

There were no chants for Mills as he entered the now-familiar Westover Ice Rink to face his great local rival on 30 March 1938. Training had gone better than ever. Turner had moved his camp to the Brunswick Hotel at Springbourne, where the publican cleared out a room especially so Freddie could prepare for one of the biggest fights Bournemouth had seen in many years.

Joining Bob Turner in the corner for this fight was Freddie's brother Charlie, who was on hand to give some insight into Lewis' boxing style having been one of the veteran's sparring partners in the past.

'Remember you're the bigger man, impose yourself,' were the final instructions from Charlie as Freddie, who outweighed Lewis by six pounds, launched himself at the crowd favourite. In front of 3,000 fans, Freddie went to work hooking away with both hands at head and body.

As in the first fight, Lewis boxed coolly and calmly, using his defensive skills to keep Freddie at bay. In the first two rounds, for all his efforts, Mills had problems penetrating the high guard Lewis employed to good effect, just as he had in their previous meeting.

Once again, much of the early action was spoiled by Lewis' habit of falling into a clinch. Having anticipated this in his sparring sessions with Charlie, Freddie effectively nullified this tactic with some crushing right uppercuts, which made Lewis visibly wince.

Realising it was pointless to try and smother Mills, Lewis began attacking Freddie's body with some clever inside work, throwing in a few uppercuts of his own. The fight burst into life in the fifth round. Impressed by Freddie's blood-and-guts performance, a large section of the crowd started to get behind the younger fighter.

Fearing Freddie could run out of steam like he did in the first fight, Bob Turner told Freddie to utilise his superior reach to box on the outside. In the latter rounds, Lewis was having to ride some of Freddie's heavier punches as a small cut appeared under the older man's eye.

A torrid tenth round left Lewis a desperate man. The accumulation of right hooks from Freddie's fists had made Lewis's left ear painfully swollen. Needing a knockout, Lewis came out for the 11th with all guns blazing. A huge left hook landed on Freddie's jaw and temporarily stopped the younger man dead in his tracks.

Responding with some vicious punches of his own, Freddie went after his man, who was more than happy to stand there and trade. The sight of the two gladiators throwing everything at each other brought the capacity crowd to their feet. Both fighters were tiring fast but neither was willing to give an inch. It was a relief when the final bell sounded to bring the full-blooded contest to an end.

'I think you just shaded it there, Fred. Well done, you'll go far,' Jack Lewis whispered to Freddie as they embraced at the end of the fight. The loud ovation from the crowd as the referee awarded Freddie the decision re-established him as a fan favourite. Back at Terrace Road, as Freddie celebrated with his family, he declared that night had been the best of his career so far.

Underneath the cover of the newly erected boxing booth just outside Bournemouth town centre, Sam McKeowen was adamant. 'There is absolutely no way I am taking him back on the booth. He's unreliable and disruptive.' Both Turners hoped McKeowen would let bygones be bygones and allow Freddie back on the booths.

After beating Lewis, Freddie became hot property in the south-west. His fame had reached as far afield as South Wales, with offers coming in from promoters in Cardiff to headline boxing bills there. The Turners hoped to cash in as quickly as possible by offering locals the chance to share the ring with Bournemouth's favourite fighter. The only sticking point was Sam.

From the moment he joined the McKeowens' boxing booth, Freddie had been nothing but trouble. He was full of himself before he beat Jack Lewis, so now he was going to be unbearable. There was nothing the manager could say to change the booth owners' minds.

Reaching into his inside jacket pocket, Bob handed Sam a ticket to a boxing show billed as Bournemouth's greatest bank holiday attraction, an evening of boxing at Boscombe Football Ground, Dean Court, where Freddie would battle with London middleweight Moe Moss. Sam asked Bob why he had given him the ticket. Turner told McKeowen to come along and experience the crowd reaction to Freddie, then tell him he wasn't worth giving a second chance.

Even though Freddie was second on the bill to a light-heavyweight contest between Eddie Pierce and Darky Ellis, there was no doubt who the audience paid to see. From the very first contest onwards, a chant of 'We want Freddie' went up. The excitement to see the local hero was almost at fever pitch when Freddie emerged for the bout, looking mean and hungry.

The walk to the ring, during which Freddie was once again accompanied by his brother Charlie and the ever-dependable Bob Turner, took an age. There were so many people who wanted to reach out and touch Freddie. It seemed everyone who was close enough to the fighter either wanted to slap him on the back or wish him well.

Wanting to keep his focus, Freddie ignored everyone. He only had his opponent on his mind. Moss was a terrific puncher who had mixed it with nearly every middleweight of note in Britain. Claiming his scalp would mean Freddie would be well placed to chase the British title.

Once inside the ring, Bob Turner looked out over the crowd. He wanted to make sure Sam McKeowen was there to see the spectacle. Sure enough the booth owner was sat in the front row, among the mayhem.

Both Charlie and Bob had been hugely impressed with Freddie's body punching. They had seen how some of the blows he delivered in the fight with Jack Lewis physically winded his opponent. In sparring with Charlie, Freddie had been urged to work the body. Such was his power, the elder Mills brother was sure Freddie had broken his ribs on several occasions when sparring.

As the first bell rang, Freddie rushed to meet Moss in the centre of the ring. After a minute and half of the first round, it was clear what Freddie's main tactic of the evening was going to be. Looking to take away his opponent's power, Mills began to open up on the body. A hard right hook to the side of Moss' head was followed by two painful-looking shots to the ribs as Freddie took the round with aplomb.

In the second, Moss decided to fight fire with fire. He went toe to toe with Freddie, with both exchanging powerful-looking left hooks. A right to the body soon took the wind out of the Londoner's sails and another left-right combination from Freddie saw Moss complain to the referee about low blows.

There were more protests in the third round when Freddie again attacked the body. The referee saw nothing wrong with Freddie's shots and told Moss off for moaning. Another exchange saw Mills cover up for the first time, although on most judges' cards Freddie had taken the first three rounds.

There was a change of tactics at the beginning of the fourth, with Freddie deciding to focus exclusively on body punching. Knowing he could not take much more of Mills' hurtful shots, Moss tried to turn the bout into a slugfest. A brief flurry of punches saw the Londoner come off worse, visiting the floor for the first time in the bout.

Confusion reigned as the referee had to inform the timekeeper that Moss had actually been knocked down. Precious seconds were wasted but the London fighter was in such a bad way he only just managed to beat the count. On rubbery legs, Moss hung on to Mills for all he was worth to see out the round.

Within 30 seconds of the start of the fifth, Moss' manager was on the ring apron screaming, 'Come on referee, that was never a knock down. He hit him in the nuts!' The referee ignored the protests and continued to count out Moss, who had been felled by an almighty right hook in the pit of the stomach. No one else watching thought it was a low blow.

With his hands in the air, Mills acknowledged the cheers of the crowd. If there had been any doubt before, there was none now. Freddie was the most popular boxer in Bournemouth, if not the south-west.

Sitting there impassively, Sam McKeowen was impressed. In the morning, he was due to meet with the Turner brothers. He had decided to take Freddie back but first wanted assurances. He wanted Mills to sign a contract whereby he would fight exclusively on the booths for two months. In that time, he would not appear on a boxing bill anywhere, not even for an exhibition. If people wanted to see Freddie Mills, they could either face him themselves in the ring or pay to see him at the McKeowen Family Boxing Booth.

After reluctantly agreeing to the terms, Bob went around to see Freddie at his mother's house. 'Fuck McKeowen,' he said. 'I want to go back with Chipperfield's.' Unbeknown to Bob Turner, Freddie had been in regular contact with Gypsy Daniels, who told him his old employer would welcome him back with open arms, especially given the level of fame he was now enjoying.

Repeating what Daniels had told him about Chipperfield's being a more famous name who paid better money than the McKeowens, Freddie told Bob that unless Sam stumped up more cash he would not be joining him at the booth this summer. The only reason Freddie had not already gone back to Chipperfield's was because of the loyalty he felt towards the Turner brothers.

After they readily agreed to match whatever wages Chipperfield's had offered him, Freddie made even more demands. He wanted time to train every morning, he would only appear if he was guaranteed a bed for the night and, above all, he wanted Sam McKeowen to acknowledge the fact that Freddie did not work for him and could not tell him what to do.

All Bob could promise to do was put this proposal to Sam McKeowen. At first, Sam was incredulous. He had been running booths for years and there was no way he was going to have terms dictated to him by any boxer.

Coming to a compromise, Bob asked Sam to take Freddie on a two-week trial. If it didn't work out, they could shake hands and move on. It quickly became clear that Freddie and Bob had McKeowen over a barrel. Such was the clamour to see Freddie that Ma McKeowen reported record takings in the first week, when they were pitched in Bournemouth.

By the time the fairground arrived at Boscombe the following week, Ma was turning people away as they queued for hours to see the Bournemouth fighter in action. Whatever problems Freddie had caused Sam McKeowen in the past were quickly forgotten in the wake of the money he was now making out of him. The other lads on the booth were happy for Freddie to be there as the large crowds he attracted brought huge amounts of nobbins for them.

Everyone seemed happy that summer, except for Freddie. As the summer wore on, life on the boxing booth was beginning to lose its appeal.

6

Enough is enough

'HE could not have been no more than 17. He may even have been much younger,' Bob Turner thought as they carried him out of the ring. He was bleeding from his ear, his white vest was covered in blood from a nasty head wound and, worryingly, he had not made a sound since he crashed to the floor in a crumpled mess.

'He's not coming round, Freddie. Fucking hell, I don't think he's breathing,' a panicked Bob told Freddie as he knelt to tend to the unfortunate young man lying on a makeshift stretcher in a private tent outside the boxing marquee. 'What the fuck were you thinking?'

Only ten minutes beforehand, the boy had been part of a rowdy group of blokes goading the booth boxers as they stood, waiting for a challenge. 'Blow us a kiss girls,' was one of the more polite retorts.

Since pitching up in Bude, Cornwall, the fighters had to put up with all sorts of comments, ranging from petty name calling to questions about their sexuality. Finally, Freddie snapped and launched himself among the crowd.

'I have had a fucking gutful of you and your mates,' Freddie snarled at the most raucous of the lads, who had been baiting him. Grabbing the loudmouth by the throat, Freddie cocked his fist ready to smash him in the face. It was Jack Turner who stopped him.

Getting between the two, Jack pushed Freddie back shouting, 'In the ring, we settle our differences in the ring.'

After some encouragement from his mates, the young man was soon stripped to the waist, ready to face Freddie. As Turner, acting as referee, brought them together for the final instructions, Freddie could smell the familiar stench of stale beer and cigarettes on the young man's breath. It seemed everyone who got in the ring with him these days were big men after a bellyful of booze.

'Go on, beat the shit into him. Smash him up,' the boy's pals yelled as they took their seats in the front row. As he waited for the bell to ring, Freddie could see the boy was having second thoughts about facing him, but he didn't care. He was determined to show the boy and his mates just how wrong they were to mess with him.

There was no subtlety about Freddie tonight. He was going to knock the boy into the middle of next week. The boy came forward but before he could throw a punch Freddie caught him with a massive left hand. The young man sagged against the ropes but Freddie was not satisfied. He wanted to hurt this boy.

As quick as a gazelle, Freddie leapt in, throwing rights and lefts until he was practically sitting on the boy's chest pounding his face, long after he could protect himself. All the while, Freddie was shouting, 'Take that, you fucker.'

'Hey, that's it. The boy's had enough,' Bob cried, using every ounce of strength he could muster to get his boxer away from his unfortunate victim.

It was only a matter of time before Freddie handed out a pasting to someone. He was into his third year on the boxing booths and was getting sick and tired of facing the drunks who wanted to impress their girlfriends or the local hard men who turned up once they knew the fair was in town.

By the time Freddie stepped into the ring with the young man, he felt he was going nowhere fast. He had learned as much as he could from the booth. He had seen how people like Tommy Farr had graduated to fighting Joe Louis for the heavyweight title and wondered when it was going to happen for him.

He feared ending up like his old friend Gypsy Daniels, becoming a journeyman fighter. A pair of losses to George Davis in August and October 1938, together with a draw with Ginger Dawkins just before Christmas, convinced him the booth was getting in the way of serious training.

Then there were the injuries. He had broken his right hand at least three times and sported a cauliflower ear and a busted nose. After a night in the booth, a frustrated Freddie, who had recently recovered from a bout of dermatitis – something he swore he caught from dirty water on the fair – spoke to Bob Turner.

'I need to be able to train and fight some decent opponents, Bob.' Agreeing to give Freddie time off in the mornings to do his roadwork and hit the heavy bag, Bob told Freddie he had lined up a fight with former Northern Area middleweight champion Charlie Parkin. It was a real opportunity for Freddie to test himself.

After weeks of hard training, Mills finally made the boxing community sit up and take notice. Coming in fitter than ever before thanks to five-mile runs and a couple of rounds on the heavy bag every morning, Freddie launched himself headlong into the action in the first round, throwing dangerous-looking lefts and right hooks to the body.

Parkin tried to dance away from his bull-like opponent, connecting with a few right hands on the more aggressive Mills. A good left hand to the body saw Freddie shake his head and smile as if to say it didn't hurt.

In the second round, Parkin began by throwing an impressive volley of punches to Freddie's midsection. It proved to be Parkin's best action of the night as Freddie stepped up a gear, throwing a vicious right cross that opened a cut above the eye of the champion.

With blood streaming from his injury, Parkin tried mixing it with Freddie in the third round. Apart from bringing the crowd at the Westover Ice Rink to their feet, this tactic did little to help Parkin's cause. A peach of a left hook connected flush with Parkin's jaw, sending him crashing to the canvas. It was all too much for the referee, who stepped in to stop the fight.

The crowd booed on hearing the result. Jack Turner told those assembled, 'If anybody doubts the gravity of this cut, I will donate £50 to the hospital right now.'

Boxing News were so impressed that they told readers there was little doubt Freddie was destined for high honours and awarded him the fight of the month.

After collecting the award and a small cheque, Freddie was sure big fights were just around the corner. He even dared to dream that the British light-heavyweight champion Jock McAvoy could be tempted to climb into the ring with him.

Then, for weeks, there was very little. Routine fights against names like Tom Curran and Johnny Blake did nothing to further his case for a fight against McAvoy. By the summer, the Turners were keen to see Freddie back on the booths.

All week, Freddie had been in a bad mood. He could not believe that only a few months earlier he was imagining a fight for the British title. Now he was putting up with abuse from anyone who fancied their chances. His frustration had bubbled over with that boy. He anxiously paced around the tent, hoping his victim would wake up. He feared the consequences if he didn't.

Recently, Freddie had read in the newspapers about the Chinese boxer Jerry Wang. One of his opponents had died in the ring and he had been charged with manslaughter. As Bob worked hard to bring the boy around, Freddie was sure the same fate awaited him.

It was another 20 minutes before the boy began groaning. Within half an hour, he was sitting up sipping on a brandy apologising to Freddie for the name calling. 'It's okay, son, boxing's a hard game. We all got to learn that lesson some time.' Freddie smiled and winked at the teenager.

The following day, Bob Turner confronted Freddie. 'You could have killed that young lad last night, what's the matter with you?'

'Bob, I am done with the booths. I've had enough of messing around. I want some real action. If you can't get me some decent fights, I will find someone who will.'

'Okay, Freddie, no more booths. Leave it with me. I will see what I can do.'

A couple of days later, Bob asked Freddie how he felt about facing Dave McCleave, who was a former British welterweight champion. The Battersea man had victories over several of Freddie's former victims and more importantly had been in with Jock McAvoy. It was a real test and Freddie was chomping at the bit.

The fight, though, was a disappointment.

From the first bell, it was Freddie who was on the back foot. McCleave used a well-schooled left jab to keep Mills at bay and relied on a heavy right hook to the body whenever the Bournemouth man rushed in.

There was a glimmer of hope in the second round when a strong left hook from Freddie caught McCleave over the eye, seeming to momentarily stun the former champion.

In the third round, the referee broke the fighters up to warn Freddie about the use of his head, which drew a loud jeer from the partisan crowd, who were firmly on Freddie's side and loudly cheered every time he landed a punch.

By the middle rounds it was clear to those watching that Freddie was unable to get on the inside, where he did his best work. It seemed for every punch Mills connected with, the wily McCleave slipped three. Of the two men, McCleave was the faster, with Freddie having to counter the straight left that was piercing his guard.

Feeling the pace, McCleave began to slow down after the seventh. Boxing defensively, he began smothering Freddie, stopping him from getting any punches off on the inside.

In the ninth, a hard right hook from Freddie landed high on the side of his opponent's head, which temporarily wobbled his legs. Going in for the kill, Freddie threw a barrage of hooks and jabs. Another right hook to the head and the crowd were on their feet sensing a shock. It was not to be. Summoning all his experience, McCleave held on to Freddie to see out the round.

In the last three rounds, Freddie would not give up. Looking for the knockout, he launched a ferocious body attack in the hope he would find the punch that would fell the former champion. It never came. Boxing coolly, McCleave kept pumping his straight left into Freddie's face while tying him up at close range.

By the end, McCleave ran out a clear winner on points. 'That's was one hell of a fight, mate. Fancy doing it again?' McCleave asked Freddie. There was only one answer but next time, Freddie thought to himself, it would be his hand raised in victory.

While awaiting a rematch with McCleave, Freddie signed to fight Nat Franks.

In this fight, Freddie came out looking to make a statement, throwing good lefts and rights to head and body from the first bell. Pushing Franks to the ropes late in the round, Freddie looked like he was in for an early night until Franks stung him with a left hand just as he was swarming all over his man.

In the second, Franks started brightly, getting home with some good lefts that knocked Mills off his stride. Shrugging off Franks' good early work, Mills began scoring with two-fisted bursts to the body. The fight followed much the same pattern in the third, with Franks making the better start of the two only to be pegged back by Freddie's unrelenting body punching.

The bout came to life in the fourth, with Freddie landing at will to body and face, and Franks showing some cute defensive skills. However, by the fifth, Franks' face was showing the effects of Freddie's punches. During the interval, his eyes were looking swollen and puffy.

In the seventh, Freddie looked to press home his advantage. He started strongly with some crisp, clean punches but as the round developed his work became ragged. He missed with some wild shots as Franks employed some crafty footwork to stay out of range. In the eighth, Freddie was firmly on top, causing damage with short uppercuts that forced Franks to cover up.

By the ninth round, Freddie looked on his way to a comfortable win. Several times, he pinned his opponent in the corner, throwing everything at him.

As the bell rang, Freddie lifted his hands in the air, certain he had won the fight. Bob Turner called him over to the corner. 'Keep going like that for the next three rounds and you'll have the fight in the bag.'

But Mills had miscounted the rounds and already given his all. A desperately tired Freddie hung on to Franks for all he was worth and was lucky to get a draw.

A rather large man waited for Freddie in his dressing room upon his return from the ring. Wearing an immaculate pin striped double breasted suit, hair slicked back and chomping on a huge cigar, the man asked if he could speak with Freddie privately.

'I watched you tonight. I liked what I saw. The crowd love you. I think I can make you a star. Have you thought about changing managers?' he asked.

Smiling, Freddie thanked him. He knew exactly who the man was. Jack Solomons was the emerging force in boxing. A former fighter under the name of Kid Mears, he ran the Devonshire Club, which staged fights for London-based boxers. At the time he was managing Eric Boon, 'The Fen Tiger', who had just became British lightweight champion and the first boxer to feature in a televised fight on the BBC.

'Come with me and I guarantee you will be facing Jock McAvoy within a few months. Jack and Bob have done well for you, but it's time to move on.'

Despite his frustrations with the Turners, Freddie still felt loyal to them. 'That's very nice, Mr Solomons, but I already have a manager.' Freddie agreed to take Solomons' card should he ever change his mind. Even though Solomons had failed to sign Freddie, he walked away impressed by his loyalty to the brothers.

Anyway, Freddie felt he did not need Solomons. After he left, the Turners told him that Dave McCleave had been as good as his word and there would be a rematch. In the weeks leading up to the bout, Freddie was meticulous about his preparation. This was his big chance. If he beat a name like McCleave, he was sure Jock McAvoy's people would come calling.

Entering the Sportsdrome, Southampton, on the night of the fight, Freddie was determined to make his mark. During training, all he had thought about was Dave McCleave. He had gone over and over their last fight in his head a thousand times. Now he was face to face with the man again.

'You will never beat McCleave if you go toe to toe. You tried that last time and it didn't work,' Bob Turner told Freddie in the build-up to the fight. He believed Freddie needed to box McCleave in the first four rounds before coming on strong in the middle of the fight.

In the end, the crowd never got to see Freddie's new style. Bouncing on the balls of his feet, Freddie could not wait to get started. After an early exchange in which it looked as though both fighters were feeling their way, McCleave reached out to throw a lazy left jab, momentarily exposing his jaw. That was the only opportunity Freddie needed and he seized it with a pulverizing right hook that landed on the button.

McCleave wilted on the ropes. A left thrown with perfect timing connected with the solar plexus, helping the former British welterweight champion on his way to the floor. As the referee counted the helpless McCleave out, Freddie announced his arrival on the British boxing scene. *Boxing News* later described Freddie's performance as having 'a touch of greatness' about it.

Freddie stood there in amazement. It was only when Bob Turner rushed over to embrace him in a huge bear hug that it dawned on Freddie that he was indeed the victor. He was now closer than ever to a fight with Jock McAvoy.

That night, as Freddie celebrated with Bob over ice cream sodas, he looked forward with a renewed opportunism. It was misplaced. The world was preparing to go to war and Freddie was about to be conscripted into the Royal Air Force (RAF). Boxing, for the time being, would have to take a back seat.

7

War!

THE commanding officer stood up behind his desk. In his hand was a piece of paper. Freddie was sure he had been called into the office for a dressing down. He had been late returning to camp from a trip to Pontypool, South Wales, where he had taken part in a booth fight.

It had been a frustrating year since his conscription into the RAF. His papers had arrived over the Christmas period telling him to report for duty in the New Forest on New Year's Day 1940.

Things had got off to a terrible start. Freddie had been laid low with pneumonia for two weeks and joined the physical instructors' course a fortnight behind everyone else. For the third time, Freddie fell off the high beam. This time, he landed face-first on the hard floor of the gymnasium, opening an old boxing wound over his eyebrow.

As the blood trickled down his face, Freddie snapped. Turning to the lecturer, he shouted, 'Fuck this. You can stick the course and the RAF up your arse.' Soon, he was storming out of the drill hall.

The blow-up had been coming for a few weeks. Freddie found the written work so difficult that he completely ignored it. The lectures were so complicated that he often found himself daydreaming when he should have been concentrating on lessons.

Even though he was a professional boxer, he was not blessed with all that much athletic ability. Parallel bars, wall bars, ropes and rings were all alien to someone more used to heavy bags and speed balls.

The only highlight of the course was the presence of Tommy Reddington, a heavyweight boxer from Salford who Freddie had got to know on the boxing booths. In the evenings, they would spar together and share stories about the people they had in common. If it had not been for Tommy, Freddie would not have lasted as long as he did on the course.

Sat in his quarters, Freddie seethed. He had pulled a muscle on the high bars when he first started and now the cut. He punched his locker in temper. It was Tommy who came looking for him.

'Let's have a look at that cut, Fred.'

'I've had it, Tommy. They'll have me breaking my neck next. This is too dangerous a life for me. I would rather go down the mines than do this any longer.'

'Come on, Freddie, get through this course and it's money for old rope,' Tommy argued.

Reddington asked Freddie to give it a week and offered to help him with the coursework. If it still didn't work, then he could walk away knowing he had given it his best shot. After some thought, Freddie agreed. After all, he did not have that many options.

Over the next month, boxing training gave way to extra gymnastic sessions in the evenings. Freddie kept up with the course work, although none of the lecturers ever thought to question why Freddie was handing in his assignments in Tommy's handwriting.

At the passing out parade, Freddie jokingly handed his PT wings to Tommy. 'Here mate, you deserve them more than me,' he told his old friend.

Things did not improve much when Freddie was posted at Netheravon in Wiltshire. Life was mundane. Apart from the morning drill, there was very little to occupy Freddie's time except for the occasional cup of tea with the lads down at the snack bar.

The only highlight was the presence of lightweight boxer Duggie Bygrave at the camp. The two became firm friends and despite the size difference took part in some full-blooded sparring sessions to keep fit and entertain some of the lads.

Despite the best efforts of Bob Turner, fights had been hard to come by. The nation was at war and potential opponents were in uniform fighting for king and country – although this didn't mean Freddie was completely inactive. He scored wins over leading contenders Ginger Sadd and Ben Valentine, which would have seen him challenge for the British title in any other year.

After Freddie dominated Fujian middleweight champion Valentine, who retired with a cut eye after three rounds, Bob Turner was sure the next time Freddie entered the ring his opponent would be Jock McAvoy. Returning to camp, Freddie could not wait to face off against the British champion.

He was to be disappointed. Weeks turned into months and there was no contact from Bob. Although regular runs along Salisbury Plain and sparring with Duggie and the boys on the camp kept him fit, it was no substitute for real boxing. Freddie wanted action.

After noticing an advertisement for a boxing booth in Pontypool, Freddie wrote to the owner asking if he wanted to book him as the star attraction. Soon, Freddie and Duggie, after being granted two days leave, hitchhiked to South Wales. The pay and the opponent, Trevor Burt, were both well below the level Freddie was used to, but it meant he could shake off some of the ring rust.

After a quickfire one-round knockout, Freddie and Duggie were soon sticking out their thumbs looking for a lift back to Wiltshire. They arrived just after lights out, a couple of hours after their leave had expired.

The CO greeted Freddie with a smile. 'Ah, Mills, come in. How was South Wales? I heard you did very well. Please take a seat.' Freddie was confused. He was sure he was in trouble.

The CO then read from the piece of paper in his hand. It was a telegram from Bob Turner asking the CO whether the RAF would grant Freddie leave to travel to Liverpool. There, he would face British middleweight champion Jock McAvoy.

A fight against McAvoy was one he had dreamed about since he was a youngster. After years of disappointment, it was finally going to happen. Freddie listened as the CO read the rest of the telegram. It was to be a non-title fight for the sum of £50. Freddie did not care about the purse. He was finally going to share the ring with one of the best-known boxers in the land.

Preparations would begin immediately, with Duggie given time off to train Freddie. No stone was left unturned. Some days, Freddie would work so hard in sparring that he would throw up in a ringside bucket between rounds before going back for more. Over and over again, Duggie would pound a ten-pound medicine ball into Freddie's midsection until bright red welts appeared on his stomach.

The pain had to be endured. Rochdale's Jock McAvoy was a hard man. Known as a knockout artist and fearsome body puncher, he had destroyed the reigning world middleweight champion Babe Risko in one round in a non-title fight in New York in 1935. Such was his dominance that Risko's handlers refused to offer him a rematch.

Upon his return to Britain in 1939, McAvoy challenged Len Harvey for the vacant British light-heavyweight title. A brutal fight in front of 90,000 fans at the White City Stadium saw McAvoy floor Harvey in the second round before nearly ending the bout in the 14th, only to lose a close 15-round decision. It turned both fighters into household names.

As tough outside the ring as he was inside, McAvoy loved to fight. It was said he would take his rage out on both men and women, and the dirtier it got the better. There was no doubt that Freddie was in for one of the roughest nights of his professional career.

Even though the RAF were happy to grant Freddie leave, they stopped short of providing transport as the war had caused a petrol shortage. So, with the biggest bout of his career looming, Freddie and Duggie, who had agreed to work his friend's corner, were once again on the side of a Wiltshire road trying to flag down a lift to Merseyside.

Once there, Freddie felt physically sick. The Liverpool Stadium was huge, far bigger than anywhere else he had fought before. 'Think I am up to this, Bob?' Freddie asked his manager, who had travelled ahead to book rooms and finalise the arrangements. 'Yeah, of course. You're going to be a world champ, mark my words.'

It was the first time anyone had ever mentioned a world championship to him. Freddie was wracked with doubt. He thought about McAvoy, who had been in with all the big names. Freddie was just a booth fighter from Bournemouth. Could he really beat him? Soon enough, he would have his answer.

Regardless of the result on 8 August 1940, Freddie had finally arrived in the big time. In the dressing room, an official from the British Boxing Board of Control watched for the first time in Freddie's career as Duggie carefully wrapped his hands. After a quick round of shadow boxing, a buzzer went off signifying that the master of ceremonies was ready to announce both fighters.

Finally, the moment Freddie had dreamed of since he was a kid boxing with his mates on the streets of Bournemouth had arrived. He was face to face with Jock McAvoy. Sensing the young fighter's nerves, the veteran grinned, 'Don't worry kid, I will go easy on you.'

If McAvoy thought Freddie would be a pushover, he was gravely mistaken. From the first bell, Freddie was like an unleashed tiger, forcing McAvoy to hang on after being rocked by a big right in the opening salvo.

Swarming all over his prey, Freddie ensured McAvoy was not able to settle into the fight. By the middle of the bout, McAvoy had decided to fight fire with fire, going toe to toe with Freddie. It was now the type of fight Mills relished – a real slugfest.

The final round brought the Liverpool crowd to their feet. Chanting 'Freddie, Freddie, Freddie', it was clear the northern crowd had adopted Mills as their favourite. As the bell rang for the 12th and final round, both fighters were determined to knock each other out. In an explosive session, both boxers threw any finesse out of the window as they tried in vain to end the fight.

'Come on, kid, keep punching, you can do better than this,' McAvoy snarled at Freddie. This only made Mills more determined to conquer his opponent. 'How do you like that for size?' Mills asked McAvoy as the Rochdale man let out a cry after taking a vicious right hook to the body. Yet the knockdown never came as the bell signalled the end of an exhilarating contest.

'Well, how did I do?' Freddie asked Duggie. Before he could reply, the referee was raising his hand as the victor. The first person to congratulate him was Jock McAvoy, 'My, my, you are a hard puncher, son. You'll go far. Well done.'

According to the newspapers the following day, a star had been born. There was excited talk of Freddie facing the British light-heavyweight champion Len Harvey. However, having waited years to challenge McAvoy, he was not prepared to wait as long for Harvey. Things were going to have to change.

8

Moving on upwards

IT was an early autumn morning when the letter arrived in the post with a Wiltshire postmark. It had been sitting on the mantelpiece for a few hours waiting for Bob Turner to return from work and he quickly opened it. It was from Freddie.

Its contents came as no surprise. In his familiar scrawl, Freddie was writing to formally request that Bob release him from his managerial contract.

Ever since Freddie beat Jock McAvoy, Bob had been expecting this. Freddie's headline-grabbing performance had put him in big demand. At every venue he fought at, it seemed he was being approached by some two-bit hustler who would promise him untold fame and fortune if only he would sign a managerial contract with them.

After watching Freddie detach the hapless Jack Powell from his senses in one short round, Ted Broadribb, wrapped in a grey overcoat and wearing a homburg hat, knew he had to be very careful about when he made his approach.

'See that shot he threw, he has the best left hook in the country,' Broadribb exclaimed to Nat Seller, the man who trained his fighters.

'Just hear that crowd ... they are red hot for him. You know what I smell, don't you?'

'Money?' Nat Seller laughed. He had seen that look in Ted Broadribb's eyes before. Freddie was his man and he was going to go all out to get him.

Both Broadribb and Seller were there on the advice of Jack Solomons, who was now more focused on promotion than managing fighters. 'I saw this kid against Nat Franks and you should see what he did to Dave McCleave. I am telling you, he could be the heavyweight champion of the world,' Solomons told Broadribb before Freddie even signed to face McAvoy.

Having never really heard of Mills, Broadribb, who had previously boxed under the name of Young Snowball and now had a stable of fighters, did not take much notice of Solomon's advice. He had had dealings with the Turner brothers in the past. Tommy Farr, who had taken the world heavyweight champion Joe Louis the distance in 1939, had appeared on booths owned by the brothers.

As Freddie won plaudits throughout the country for his performance, Bob Turner knew it was only a matter of time before Freddie would have his head turned by a manager with better connections. Freddie was no longer the novice 16-year-old boy he had met in Bournemouth all those years ago. He was now knocking on the door of a British title challenge. He knew Ted Broadribb was not in the audience that night for the Powell fight simply to be entertained.

'You going to make a move, Ted?' Seller enquired. 'Not yet, I need to check out a few things,' replied Broadribb.

Through contacts at the British Boxing Board of Control, Broadribb discovered that Freddie had a rolling one-year contract with Turner, which could be bought out at any time for the sum of £200. Crucially, he learned that Bob had hoped to join the RAF and wanted out of the fight game.

While Bob knew Freddie was too great a talent not to move on, he was not going to let him move to just anyone. He had known Freddie for five years and was very protective of him. Once Broadribb approached him about Freddie's contract, Bob wanted assurances he would look after his fighter. Broadribb told Turner he would treat him like one of the family.

'That was fantastic,' Broadribb told a disappointed Freddie, who was surprised to find the manager waiting for him on his return to his dressing room after a lack-lustre performance against his old friend and PT course alumni Tommy Reddington. 'No it wasn't, I was shit,' grumbled Freddie. 'I was lucky to get the decision.'

'You know what you need, don't you?' asked Broadribb rhetorically. 'Fights that will motivate you. You need to be where the action is – London. That's where all the big fights are. I can make it happen. Are you under contract?'

Freddie had no idea Broadribb had already discussed his future with Bob Turner.

Initially, Freddie's reply was the same as he had given Jack Solomons years earlier. Thank you very much but he already had a manager. Then Broadribb caught him unawares. 'Yes, but Bob Turner won't be around much longer. Everyone knows he's off to the RAF. Then where will you be? No manager means no fights.'

Freddie knew Bob had plans for a life in the forces but secretly hoped he would shelve them to continue managing him.

Before Freddie could reply, the door opened and Turner entered. Taking his cue, Broadribb extended his arm to shake

Freddie's hand, then bid him good night. 'Been sniffing around, has he?' Bob asked Freddie. 'Look, it's up to you. He fixed [sic] Tommy Farr's world title fight with Joe Louis at the New York Yankees' stadium, and he could be good for you.' Freddie agreed to sleep on it.

There was no doubt he wanted the biggest fights, but he felt a loyalty to Bob and Jack Turner. After all, they had given him a start in boxing. Without them, Freddie was sure he would still have been getting the horses ready for the morning milk round at the dairy or doing any one of the mundane jobs his friends had back home in Bournemouth.

Sleep did not come easy to Freddie that night. He knew he had a big decision to make: stay with Bob and hope the Len Harvey fight would somehow materialise or go after the big matches in London. He thought back to when he felt he was on the road to nowhere in the boxing booth a few summers ago, reading about the exploits of Jimmy Wilde and Tommy Farr, and wondering whether he was ever going to follow them into the big time. Now he had the opportunity to follow their path and it scared him.

Any thoughts of delaying a decision would soon not be an option anyway. The following morning, after drilling the boys, Freddie returned to his quarters to be told he had a visitor. It was Ted Broadribb, who had travelled all the way down from London.

He was determined to sign Freddie. It was not going to be a wasted journey. This time, he was not going to take no for an answer. He was going to walk away with Freddie's signature on a managerial contract. 'First, we get McAvoy in a re-match as an eliminator for the British light-heavyweight crown, then we take on Len Harvey,' he promised Freddie.

'I told Tommy Farr I would get him Joe Louis and I am telling you the same. Freddie, you can go one better and be the heavyweight champion of the world.'

For the past few months, Freddie had been dreaming of facing Len Harvey, but Joe Louis? That was beyond his wildest dreams and Ted Broadribb was telling him he could make it happen.

Finally, Broadribb sealed the deal by alleviating Freddie's fears about the Turner brothers. 'I know you have been with them a long time. They will understand. If you sign with me, I will treat you like the son I never had. You will be practically family.'

Before beginning his journey back to London, Broadribb stopped to post a letter in the small village of Netheravon. It was written by Freddie under the guidance of Broadribb and addressed to Bob Turner, effectively ending their managerial arrangement. The last business Turner ever undertook with Freddie was to grant him his wish and accept the £200 on offer from Broadribb to buy out Freddie's contract.

But things did not start particularly well. His first fight under Broadribb's guidance was a disaster. He was disqualified for a low blow in the third round of a bout against Jack Hyams, which Freddie put down to nerves as he was so eager to please his new manager.

Three weeks later, he was due to box again. Freddie mulled over his progress as he finished a training session and began stretching. He needed to make a statement but as he bent to touch his toes he felt something pop in the small of his back. It was the last thing he needed.

On 29 September 1941, Broadribb had booked him on to a bill at the Royal Albert Hall, where he would take on dangerous heavyweight Tommy Martin. It was a way of introducing him to a London audience. Freddie's fight with McAvoy had dominated the newsreels and Broadribb was sure the capital's fight fans would come out in droves to see Britain's new boxing superstar in the flesh. But the day before the fight, while skipping to warm up, Freddie stiffened. The training injury had returned.

'Ted, my back's gone there is no way I can fight.' Mills said, wincing.

'You can forget that nonsense when you like. There is a lot riding on this,' snapped Broadribb.

Telling his new charge of a masseur who could work miracles, Broadribb told Freddie there was no way he could cancel. When the massage did not work, Broadribb took it upon himself to run an ultra violet lamp over Freddie's injured back.

Not wanting to let his new manager down, Freddie told Broadribb he felt fine on the morning of the fight. He was lying. It had taken him nearly an hour to get out of bed and he was having trouble walking.

Before the first bell rang, Freddie sat on the stool almost unable to move, with the fanfare of the organ that greeted his arrival still ringing in his ears. He wondered how he would react to the first shot he took and hoped he could end things quickly.

Understandably cautious in his approach, Freddie was shocked by the quick start made by his opponent. A hard right cross, which snapped Freddie's head back, finally awoke the beast inside him. At the end of the opening round, he roared into action, his two-fisted aggression stopping the marauding Martin in his tracks.

By the second round and despite the back trouble, Freddie was firmly on top, almost knocking Martin down. Fighting through the pain, Freddie's relentless pressure saw him wear down his man in the fifth, with the referee stepping in to stop the fight. At the end, Freddie could barely lift his arms above his shoulders. When Broadribb put his arms around him in a bear hug to congratulate him, he felt like his ribs were caught in a vice.

'Who said you couldn't do it, Freddie?' a jubilant Ted asked his fighter. The adrenalin had carried Freddie through the fight. Now back in the dressing room, the pain was worse than ever. After lying on the rub-down table unable to move for over an hour, Freddie needed help getting dressed.

Three months later, Freddie found himself back at the Royal Albert Hall. The back had continued to cause him problems but hadn't prevented boxing twice more since Martin, against heavyweights Jim Wilde and Tom Reddington. Looking resplendent in new dressing gown with the initials 'FM' on the back, no one could have known the pain Freddie was in.

As Jack London bent down to tie his shoelaces, Freddie caught a glimpse of his huge shoulder muscles. If he had any hope of facing Len Harvey, Freddie had to get back to winning ways. The back had affected his last performance, in which he had dropped a decision to his old friend Reddington.

'Whatever you do, start carefully and take his measure. He's quite the puncher, son.' Broadribb advised Freddie. Watching as Freddie loosened up in the ring with some shadow boxing was Broadribb's daughter Chrissie, who was married to another Broadribb fighter, Don McCorkindale.

As the fighters got down to action, Freddie took his manager's advice and started carefully. However, in the second round, a heavy right hand from London caught Freddie in the small of the back, making the old injury flare up again. From that point until the fight's conclusion, each shot thrown by London hurt. The lower back pain was intense and Freddie was blowing heavily. Those who watched him struggle against the much bigger London felt he was lucky to nick the decision over ten rounds.

When Freddie got back to camp, he complained again of the pain in his back. Eventually, an X-ray found he had fractured a couple of ribs. Strapping him up, the doctor recommended complete rest with no heavy lifting for at least six weeks.

As soon as the bandaging came off after three weeks, early in the New Year, Freddie felt fit enough to climb back in the ring for his rubber match with Tommy Reddington. Settling matters once and for all, and showing no ill effects from the injury, Freddie pummelled the Salford man from the opening bell, catching Reddington with a solid left hook and sending him to the canvas for a count of nine. From that moment onwards, Freddie grew in confidence. In the seventh, a tiring Reddington whispered to Freddie in a clinch, 'Take it easy, Fred. I thought we were mates!'

Reddington should have known better. Friendly and affable outside the ring, Freddie was all business inside it. Ignoring his old mate's request, Freddie went about his work, breaking up Reddington's body.

Another two-fisted assault from Freddie in the ninth round and the referee had seen enough, stepping to save the stricken Reddington, who had sagged on the ropes at the mercy of Freddie's murderous punches.

By now, Freddie was a regular performer on some of British boxing's biggest stages. His reputation was growing every time he fought. The sporting press were united in their belief that he should face Len Harvey for the British and Empire light-heavyweight titles.

However, to do that he first had to win a title eliminator against old foe Jock McAvoy, which was scheduled for 23 February 1942. For the third time in a row, Freddie fought at the Royal Albert Hall and yet he was worried. He was struggling to get the weight off in time for the fight.

Nothing he did had worked. Ever since the fight was signed, he had not eaten anything. Each day he had sat in a hot bath but he was still four pounds over the light-heavyweight limit. Freddie was miserable. He hoped meeting up with old friends Duggie Bygrave and Tommy Reddington, arriving in London from camp, would improve his mood.

After a good night, the three of them slipped away to the Jermyn Street baths. Stripping off for a massage, Freddie jumped on the scales but was still four pounds overweight.

He could not take any more. An hour in the steam room and Freddie felt light-headed. Coming out, he weighed in again and had lost two pounds. After another 60 minutes of heavy sweating and desperately in need of some water, Freddie achieved his target. He was bang on the light-heavyweight limit of 12st 7lbs.

A record crowd eagerly anticipated the entry of the two men, who would fight for the privilege of facing Len Harvey. Once in the ring, there was an inspection of the bandages to make sure the approved seals hadn't been tampered with, then Broadribb tossed a coin to decide who picked the gloves.

As Freddie stared across the ring at his opponent, a real tension hung in the air. Mills was no longer a kid being given an opportunity by an experienced champion. This was serious. Feeling he had been robbed by Harvey in their last fight, McAvoy wanted revenge and he was going to go through Mills to get it. Freddie, on the other hand, was keen to beat both McAvoy and Harvey and claim his place at the very top of British boxing. Those watching that night could expect fireworks.

In their last meeting in Liverpool, Freddie had come tearing out looking for an early knockout. This time he began cautiously, slowly circling around McAvoy, looking for an opening before launching his attack. It was half a minute into the round before Mills threw a left hook to the body, which caused the Rochdale man to wince and wheel away in pain.

The referee broke the fighters up and took a look at McAvoy. 'Are you okay?' he asked. The British middleweight champion nodded and put his hands up ready to fight. Freddie went back to work on the body, chucking a right and a left hook to the ribs, when McAvoy slipped before crying out, 'My back's gone, my back's gone.'

Confusion reigned. Holding his back, the tough Northerner told the referee he could not go on. Looking over to Duggie, who urged him to finish the job as no break had been called, Freddie stood dumbfounded with his arms by his sides.

The referee quickly waved the contest over, declaring Freddie the winner before helping the proud former champion McAvoy back to his stool. Boos continued to ring around the Royal Albert Hall as the punters felt ripped off by the outcome of the fight. The ring was quickly awash with strewn beer bottles.

The crowd began chanting, 'What a load of rubbish' followed by 'Fix, fix, fix'. It was an unsatisfactory ending to one of the most eagerly awaited bouts of the year. Not that Freddie cared all that much. His record showed he had beaten Jock McAvoy twice. When the press asked who he wanted his next opponent to be, he had only one name in mind: Len Harvey.

It was now up to Ted Broadribb to prove he was as good as his word.

9

Lost in the city

THE last thing Freddie could remember was jumping on a train to London. After that, it was blur. Despite having his face splashed on the front of every newspaper and hailed a national hero, he wandered around the capital city an anonymous man. He could not remember where he went, who he spoke to or where he stayed. He had vague memories of visiting Trafalgar Square and Madame Tussauds, but that was it.

Just a few days before, he was on top of the world. Now the RAF officially listed him as absent without leave. Family and friends were anxious. No one had heard from Freddie for days. His manager Ted Broadribb was at a loss to explain what had happened. He frantically tried to stave off journalists desperate to interview the new British light-heavyweight champion. However, he was nowhere to be found.

If the truth be told, Freddie had daydreamed about running away for months. After another day that finished in the early hours, he was at the end of his tether. Some days, when he had returned to camp after an exhibition with Duggie Bygrave, he was so tired he could hardly move. He could not remember the last time he had a break. Every day he was being pulled in all directions.

Freddie's day was jam packed. After drilling the boys at 7am, he spent the rest of the morning training. Afternoons were taken up coaching the Netheravon boxing team, which he had formed with some of the lads on the camp. The evenings saw Freddie travelling to nearby RAF stations putting on boxing exhibitions as a morale booster. Any leave was used so he could continue with his boxing career.

Things got so bad that Freddie spoke with his commanding officer about a move away from Netheravon. A posting to South Witham in Lincolnshire was no real improvement. The work, loading bombs on to trucks, was laborious. The long days were no longer broken up by boxing as there was no team, no Duggie Bygrave and no facilities except for a heavy bag that Freddie had hung in a civilian canteen.

Any hopes of using his accumulated two weeks' leave for a meaningful holiday were dashed when Ted Broadribb announced he had got Len Harvey's name on a contract. He had to move fast as he feared the RAF would match their two PT instructors in an exhibition. There was no way Broadribb was going to allow the two hottest properties in British boxing to meet for free.

The fight was set to be staged at White Hart Lane, home of Tottenham Hotspur Football Club. It was the biggest sporting event in the United Kingdom since the outbreak of the war. From the moment Freddie arrived from Lincolnshire to set up his training camp at the Airman pub in Feltham, he felt the pressure.

The fight could not have come at a better time for British boxing. The sport was beginning to feel the pinch of the war. Shows were staged for charity, with promoters keeping only the running expenses. Wartime restrictions on heating and electricity meant that most shows took place outside and promoters were reluctant to gamble on the weather. Rainy days meant heavy financial losses. Meanwhile, due to a shortage of paper, *Boxing News* had become little more than a one-page information sheet.

Crowds of hundreds paid six pence on the door to catch a glimpse of their hero training. All the money collected was donated to the RAF benevolent fund. For once, Freddie the exhibitionist hated people watching him. He was finding it difficult to focus his mind on the task at hand. The newspapers delivered each morning did not help his state of mind.

Interest in the media was intense. Most were dismissive of Freddie's chances. To them, Len Harvey was just too good. They asked, 'Who had Freddie beaten anyway?' His best win had been against an over-the-hill Jock McAvoy, who had never been the same fighter after tangling with Harvey. The thinking was there was no way this young upstart from Bournemouth, who only a few years before had been on the boxing booths, could possibly beat the fighting man from Cornwall.

There was little wonder why the newspapers were firmly on Harvey's side. The Cornishman had seen and done it all before. Starting out as a 12-year-old flyweight, he was one of the first British boxers to headline Madison Square Garden in New York. He won British titles at middleweight, light-heavyweight and heavyweight.

During the 1930s, Harvey was the most popular boxer in the land. In 1934, when he faced Welshman Jack Petersen for the British heavyweight title, some 90,000 people roared him on at the White City Stadium. This was matched five years later at the same venue when the British Boxing Board of Control recognised Harvey as the world champion after outpointing Jock McAvoy, although the Americans disputed this.

By the time Harvey signed to face Mills, such was his fame that his likeness hung in the National Portrait Gallery. However, unlike the press, Broadribb sensed a chink in the old champion's armour. At 35, Harvey was 12 years older than Freddie and had not been in a ring since beating McAvoy three years earlier. He was bound to be suffering from some ring rustiness.

None of this stopped boxing writers from predicting a Harvey win. As Freddie prepared to leave Feltham, he picked up the morning newspaper. 'Harvey will be the matador to Mills' bull', one back page predicted. The paper went on to remind Freddie that except for a fight that ended in his opponent's disqualification, Harvey had never been off his feet in a 22-year career.

Sat in the front seat of the car, Broadribb could see Freddie's hand trembling as he read about his predicted defeat against the old champion. 'Pay no attention to that crap. Harvey is an old man. No one has landed one on this geezer for years. He will not be able to handle your power, Freddie.'

After the weigh-in, returning to Broadribb's house in Shepperton, there was little Mills could do. The clock ticked more slowly than ever. He tried to lie down for an afternoon nap but could not sleep. He could not face food, such was the knot in his stomach. There was only one thing that would settle him and that was to finally stare at Harvey across the ring.

After what seemed like an age, Freddie was at the arena. As an official from the Board of Control visited to check his hand wraps, Broadribb made things worse by telling Freddie this was the biggest crowd he had seen in a long time. He estimated that most of them had come to see Freddie beat Harvey. 'Pack it in, Ted,' Freddie ordered. He wanted silence to focus his mind.

The nerves didn't dissipate as Freddie made the walk to the ring ahead of the first bell. The tension made his arms and legs feel heavy. He tried to ease the stress by breaking into a little jog before getting through the ropes. The 40,000-strong crowd erupted as he appeared. Despite his inner turmoil, Mills looked relaxed as he waved to the audience. Their cheers were drowned out by the Dagenham Girl Pipers.

Freddie danced around the ring, flicking out jabs and hooks into the summer night air. He did his best to ignore the arrival of Harvey. He was emboldened by the fact he was the bigger man, weighing in more than two pounds heavier than the champion. It was clear to those watching that Freddie had trained hard. His face looked taut and his body rock hard.

Some observers, who had not seen Len Harvey in the ring since his victory over Jock McAvoy, remarked how much he had aged once he started his own ring walk. There seemed less of a spring in his step and he avoided Freddie's icy cold stare, keeping his head down once he had climbed through the ropes.

The perceived lack of self-confidence in Harvey did not go unnoticed in his young opponent's corner. 'See? He's not the man he used to be,' Broadribb told Freddie as he massaged his shoulders. With their hands bandaged, they were called together by the referee to flip a coin to decide which gloves they wore. As Ted pulled on Freddie's gloves, he whispered, 'Good luck, Freddie.'

Broadribb felt almost as nervous as his boxer. There was a lot riding on this. If Freddie could beat Harvey, he would be recognised by the British Boxing Board of Control as world champion. On the other side of the Atlantic, American Gus Lesnevich claimed the crown for himself. Sooner or later, the two best light-heavyweights would have to meet in what was bound to be an extremely lucrative bout.

After the final instructions from the referee, the bell finally rang to start the first round. The crowd roared as Freddie rushed at Harvey. Harvey met his opponent with a straight left that momentarily jolted the head of the young challenger. In truth, it had little effect. Freddie kept coming forward, throwing punches to the body. At the end of the round, there was a trickle of blood from Harvey's nose but few thought the Cornishman had been particularly troubled. It did not matter what the watching press thought. Freddie had been encouraged by a right hook that caught Harvey square in the mouth. It had stopped the Cornishman in his tracks and forced him to hold on.

'I think I hurt him a little there, Ted,' said Freddie.

'I think you're right,' replied Broadribb. 'I told you he's not what he used to be. He'll never take 14 rounds of this.'

Little did Broadribb and Mills know that Harvey's corner was worried. In that first round, they had noticed a change in the champion. Like many greats, he had become a master at 'tying up' his man. Harvey was renowned for what *Boxing News* termed his 'gripping power', and opponents who found themselves in clinches with him would suffer from numbness in their arms as he squeezed.

The pundits felt Harvey had shaded the first round but each time he got in close he had failed to tie up Freddie in a clinch. The question had to be asked whether Freddie was just too strong for the ageing champion.

Yes, Harvey had scored with few lefts against the oncoming challenger but it was nothing Freddie wasn't used to and they had failed to trouble him. As the bell rang for the end of the first round, there was nothing to suggest the fireworks that were to come in the second.

Within the first 60 seconds of the round, Harvey learned the hardest lesson of all in boxing: that one punch can turn a boxer from a great champion into an old man, very quickly. Freddie emerged from his corner in a semi-crouch and Harvey kept him at bay with another straight left, pushing his opponent back towards his corner.

Freddie came back again looking for an opening and this time, unlike in the first round, Harvey was happy to clinch his opponent. They continued to jockey for position in the middle of the ring, throwing some blows to the body when in close.

Then came the moment that changed the whole complexion of the fight. Freddie threw a long left hook that landed cleanly on Harvey's jaw. Detached from his senses, Harvey fell heavily to the canvas and for a moment it looked as though the champion would roll through the ropes.

Ever the pro, Harvey quickly took to one knee. He waited until the count reached nine before rising to his feet. The referee took one look into Harvey's eyes and, detecting no grogginess, wiped his gloves and allowed him to continue.

Going in for the kill, the animalistic Mills assailed his prey with a volley of punches. The cunning old champion instinctively bobbed his head from side to side trying to avoid each blow.

It was to no avail as Freddie threw ten unanswered punches and Harvey sagged towards the floor. It was clear the fight was no longer competitive and another left hook brought an end to the reign of Harvey as British and Empire light-heavyweight champion.

For such a proud champion, it was a humiliating finish. The knockout punch lifted Harvey between the middle and top rope and out of the ring. He landed on the timekeeper, smashed his head on a desk and chair before rolling under the ring. The journalists who were following the fight scattered like tenpins in a bowling alley.

Valiantly, Harvey tried to climb back but it was too late. The referee had waved the contest over. In less than four minutes – three minutes and 58 seconds to be exact – Freddie Mills had become British boxing's undisputed superstar.

Pandemonium ensued. Journalists were desperate for a comment from the young fighter they had written off earlier in the day. They could wait as Freddie only wanted to speak to the man he had idolised as a kid, Len Harvey.

'I'm sorry the fight ended that way, Len,' Freddie whispered in the former champion's ear as they embraced.

'That's quite okay, champ. You were the better man.' Freddie could not believe the man he dreamt of facing as a child had just called him champ.

Having made his way through a throng of well-wishers and supporters in the crowd, Mills was met by a number of journalists who it seemed would not tire of questioning him about the fight, but the highlight of the night was eventually seeing his father Tom. He was a man of few words but the smile on his face meant there was no need for words. Tom was so proud of his son's achievement.

The following day, Freddie travelled back to his RAF camp by train. In the compartment, he saw dozens of people reading newspapers, with news of his big win on the front page. With his decisive victory over Harvey in the bag, his world was filled with all sorts of possibilities. Freddie was now acknowledged by the British Boxing Board of Control as world champion but recognition in America would only come if he beat Lesnevich, who was rumoured to be on his way to Britain in the near future with the American armed forces.

There was also the matter of the British and Empire heavyweight championship, which had been held by Harvey, although only his light-heavyweight crown had been on the line in the Mills fight. Such was the manner of Harvey's defeat that there would have been little appetite for a rematch and retirement was now on the cards. If Harvey gave up the title, the general consensus was that Freddie would be matched with Tommy Farr for the vacant crown. It would be an easy match to make, given that Ted Broadribb managed both fighters.

Once back in his quarters in Lincolnshire, Freddie held his head in his hands. The room was in darkness and he liked it that way. For the past few days, Ted plotted his next move but Freddie could take no more. News he was to move to St Athan in South Wales had unsettled him. He hated moving and found it difficult to make new friends. Each time he had moved in the past, he had wanted to leave a few days after arriving.

Since his conscription into the RAF, Freddie felt his life was out of control. The headaches and nausea he had begun to suffer on the boxing booths had become more frequent. The RAF was working him into the ground and Broadribb was full of plans for even more fights. There was no respite. He had to get away.

Before climbing on the train for London the week after the Harvey fight, Freddie told one of the corporals to cover for him. He had been given a leave pass for Saturday and decided to go early on the Friday. When Freddie did not return to camp on Monday, the corporal had no choice but to report him missing.

The commanding officer telephoned Ted Broadribb, who begged him not to begin court martial proceedings against the new British light-heavyweight champion. He was sure it was just a misunderstanding and could quickly be ironed out.

Anyone who had seen Freddie wandering through Piccadilly and Leicester Square would have taken him for a tourist, but his mind was in turmoil. He wanted everything to go back to how it used to be, before he met Ted Broadribb, to those carefree early days with Jack and Bob Turner in Bournemouth. Then, he used to fight for pleasure before it all got too much for him.

Standing on Waterloo Bridge, Freddie aimlessly threw pebbles into the Thames. In his entire life, he had never felt this low. Looking down at the murky river, he knew he could never turn the clock back. Dark thoughts entered his head. If he threw himself in, no one would miss him. Standing there, he thought of his mother and the shame it would bring to his family.

After a few days, he finally came to his senses. He reasoned he was coming down from such adulation after the Harvey fight and he was also suffering from exhaustion. He had been working 15 hours a day while also using his leave time to prepare for fights. He simply had not had any time to rest.

Upon his return, Freddie found a sympathetic commanding officer. To have the most famous sportsman in the land among their ranks was a real coup for the RAF. Rather than face a court martial, Mills was told to take his time before his move to St Athan. The RAF never mentioned the incident again and Freddie never talked about it. It was simply swept under the carpet.

Eventually, Len Harvey relinquished the British and Empire heavyweight titles and retired from boxing. Unsurprisingly, Freddie's name was mentioned as a contender for the vacancy, alongside Jack London, Bruce Woodcock and Leeds fighter Al Robinson.

However, fighting for the British heavyweight title was not the most pressing matter on Freddie's mind. His days of filling huge arenas were soon to come to a temporary close. As a serving airman, it was only a matter of time before he was sent abroad. Little did Freddie know but his posting would open up another avenue for his career.

10

Frustration

NEWS that the legendary Joe Louis was in town and interested in an exhibition bout lifted Freddie's spirits. The past year had been one of frustration. Broadribb had tried to chase down a meeting with leading contender Jack London for the vacant British heavyweight crown, but to no avail.

Time was running out. When he was told he was on the move from St Athan, he was sure his next posting would be overseas. Instead it was back to the familiar Wiltshire countryside, this time to the village of Upavon. Finding activities to keep 50 Italian prisoners of war occupied was hard work. Most days, Freddie made sure they cut down trees and did some gardening around the camp.

After the excitement of the Harvey fight, there had been an anti-climax. Thanks to the war, fights were becoming harder and harder to come by. In the 18-month period after winning the British title, he had only been matched in two fights, against the Yorkshireman Al Robinson.

Both were unsatisfactory. In their first clash, the much heavier Robinson inflicted a deep cut over Freddie's eyebrow, which had first opened up a few days earlier in training. While it bled profusely from the first round, it had little effect on the outcome, with the referee stepping in to stop Robinson taking further punishment in the sixth round.

Their rematch, at Elland Road, Leeds, was something of a farce. Freddie was carried to the ring on stablemate Don McCorkindale's back. The weather was so bad that Freddie feared the waterlogged pitch would wreck his boxing boots.

There was a huge puddle in the ring from a tear in the canopy above. It was so bad that Freddie and Robinson agreed if either of them slipped in the ring, they would stop fighting immediately and declare the bout a no contest. Mercifully for the crowd, who sought shelter under umbrellas after being soaked by the torrential rain, Freddie kept things short and sweet, dispatching Robinson easily in two rounds.

As Freddie ran back to his dressing room to celebrate his win, little did he know that would be the only time the British public would see him box in 1943. As the year wore on, Freddie began to take his frustrations out on his manager.

It was hardly Broadribb's fault. He had managed to get Jack London to sign for a fight with Freddie in September 1943. The venue had caused some controversy in the press, with many writers asking why the hero of the masses, Freddie Mills, was fighting for the British heavyweight title at the exclusive Queensbury Club in London when it could only house 2,000 people at best. Things were made worse when tickets were priced at 25 guineas, way beyond what the average working man could afford.

Freddie had set up camp on the golden mile in Brentford. His former opponent, Jim Wild, acted as chief sparring partner, while his old mate from his RAF PT course, Tommy Reddington, did the same job for Jack London.

In London's final sparring session, Reddington delivered a cracking right hook to London's body. The man from Hartlepool let out a loud cry and fell to his knees, where he remained for five minutes holding his left side. 'Argh! I think you have bust my ribs, Tommy.' A couple of hours later, it was confirmed the proposed British title fight between Mills and London had been postponed indefinitely.

The £2,000 cheque that London handed over to Freddie as compensation for cancelling their fight did very little to alter his mood. He wanted to be in with top opposition. Then, as luck would have it, the very best in the world, Joe Louis, invited Freddie to take on an American team of GIs in an exhibition competition.

Ever since Ted Broadribb had signed Freddie, he kept telling him a fight with Joe Louis at Madison Square Garden was his destiny. When they finally came face to face, it was just up the road from Upavon in the less glamourous surroundings of Bulford army camp. 'So, they tell me you are a world champ? I think Gus would have something to say about that,' Louis drawled, referring to the other man who claimed to be world light-heavyweight champion, Gus Lesnevich. Freddie just smiled.

'Hey, Mills you done this before? You know the score?' Freddie thought he was in a dream. Not only was he shaking hands with Louis but former world heavyweight champion Jack Dempsey was talking to him and about to referee one of his bouts.

'Joe's much too big for you. We are going to stick you in with a fella called Bob Scully and then finish with Leo Matricciani. Just give the boys a good show.'

The first fight with Scully went smoothly enough. Freddie never took it very seriously and neither did his opponent. At various times, they let each other pound away but it was never a real fight and Dempsey called it a draw.

Then it was Freddie's turn to meet Matricciani. There was something altogether different about him. When Dempsey pulled them together to issue the final instructions, the American looked right through Freddie with a menacing stare.

The first bell rang with Freddie pawing out two soft left jabs. Matricciani absorbed both punches before landing a crushing right on the jaw of the unsuspecting Freddie. He then followed up with a spiteful uppercut, which nearly knocked Freddie clean out.

Using all his experience, Freddie held the American in a clinch. 'What the fuck was that? It's supposed to be an exhibition,' Freddie whispered in the ear of the American.

'I am going to fuck you up. World fucking champion? You are nothing but a bum,' replied Matricciani. Trying to buy as much time as possible, Freddie held on until Dempsey intervened to break them up.

Now Freddie realised he was in a fight. For three rounds, they went at it hammer and tongs, neither willing to take a step back. As Dempsey declared another draw, Freddie felt the effects of his unexpected battle in the ring. He was suffering from double vision, which made him nauseous. He still felt ill when Ted came to visit him in camp a few days later to tell him he had a date for a fight with Jack London.

The venue was going to be the site of his greatest triumph, White Hart Lane, and the fight was all set for July 1944. Unfortunately, buzz bombs began dropping all over London and it was deemed unsafe to stage a major sporting event in the capital. When the fight was postponed again, Freddie thought he would never face off against Jack London for the titles.

'Freddie, we are off to Manchester. London has agreed to meet you there.' Broadribb assured him.

'Yeah, yeah, Ted. You're full of shit,' said Freddie, reacting to the news that King's Hall, Belle Vue, Manchester was to be the venue for the re-scheduled fight with Jack London. Even as the date grew closer, Freddie was sure there would be another postponement.

Training at Upavon was hardly intense. The RAF, keen to have the British heavyweight champion in its ranks, was very accommodating, with two sparring partners and a masseur allowed to stay on the camp.

Although he knew Freddie was very fit, Broadribb was worried his man lacked sharpness as he travelled with him to Manchester for the fight. His concern grew as Freddie told Ted of the practical jokes he and his mates had played on the Italian prisoners of war.

The press, on the other hand, was in no doubt. Freddie was going to destroy Jack London. The big man from Hartlepool was written off as slow and cumbersome. They predicted the explosive Freddie would have too much power for the flat-footed London and end the bout long before the difference in weight would begin to tell.

Looking at London at the weigh-in on the afternoon before the fight, Freddie was sure the man from the North East was even bigger than he had been in their last meeting. His huge, muscled shoulders resembled barn doors. After the scales revealed the man Freddie would be facing that night was a full 3st heavier, London struck a bodybuilder's pose. It seemed that every muscle was heavily developed.

Freddie thought he was not facing the same fighter as before. No one would turn up in that type of shape unless he had prepared thoroughly. He had spent three weeks messing around in training thinking the fight was going to be postponed and now he was worried. 'He's looking good Ted,' admitted Freddie.

'He's more a circus strongman than a boxer, Freddie. You will beat him easy.' Despite Ted's optimism, Freddie was not so sure. Jack London looked like he meant business.

Over 7,000 Mancunians packed into the King's Hall that night. They had already seen the new British heavyweight sensation Bruce Woodcock extend his unbeaten record with a ferocious display, stopping George Marwick in the third round. By the time Mills and London made their way to the ring, the northern crowd were well warmed up and expecting fireworks.

There was no doubt whose side the capacity crowd was on. 'London, London, London!' In the corner, Freddie quipped, 'I thought we were in Manchester, not London!' Broadribb told him to keep his mind on the job and save the jokes for after the fight.

When the bell finally rang for the first round, the fight began as the experts predicted. Mills charged out throwing rapid hooks, making London miss as his smaller, speedier opponent darted in and out of range. The early rounds saw Freddie land punches with ease and he quickly built up a lead in the fight.

At the end of the third, Broadribb was sure it was going to be an early night for his fighter. 'He's hitting nothing but shadows.'

However, despite Freddie throwing more shots, slowly but surely London began to gain a foothold in the bout and he fought back, landing some big punches. Freddie was still able to force London back but as the fight moved towards its latter stages London's heavier punches were doing the most damage.

Observers at ringside had Mills just shading it until the 12th round. It was from this point that the tide turned in London's favour as the energy began to sap from Freddie's body. It seemed the lack of serious training had begun to tell. Mills was blowing hard and clinching much more than he ever did throughout the early stages.

In the final three rounds, London pressed home his weight advantage, bearing down on his lighter opponent's shoulders. There was now more spite behind London's heavier punches. Each one was causing damage to Freddie's face, with a cut developing over his right eye. It was no use going toe to toe with London like he did in the earlier rounds. Survival was now the only thing on Freddie's mind as the final bell approached.

In the 13th round, still hoping to knock his lighter opponent out, London began going to the body. Two venomous right hooks, one after each other, took Freddie's breath away. Such was the pain that Mills suspected he might have broken a few ribs. The shots temporarily slowed Freddie up, making him an easy target for London's power punches, which now landed with more frequency.

'You are going to need a knockout,' Broadribb shouted at Freddie as he prepared to go out for the 14th round. Looking to grab back some of the ground, Mills went about his work, rushing at the bigger man. Before any of this had a real impact, a strong right cross sent Freddie across the ring, bringing the Manchester crowd to their feet in the hope their favourite would knock Mills out.

In the final round, it looked as though London would grant the audience's wish and claim the title with a knockout of his much smaller opponent. London was landing at will. Pinned in the corner, Mills was taking everything London threw at him. Heavy rights and lefts went in around the head and body. Demonstrating remarkable courage, Freddie hung on, moving out of the way, trying to reply with shots of his own.

In the closing minute, not wanting to end the fight on his back, Freddie used his superior speed to keep out of range, managing to avoid London's most dangerous shots. In the end, even though Freddie felt he had done enough to shade it, there were few who disagreed when the referee lifted London's arm to signify a points decision for the man from Hartlepool.

Although disappointed not to see a knockdown, the Manchester crowd would not go home disappointed. They had seen a real blood-and-guts, drawn-out contest, with *Boxing News* claiming it was the best heavyweight fight seen in a British ring for years.

'You didn't train hard enough, Freddie. We're going to have to sort you out with a decent full-time trainer. You've got to stop messing around.' Broadribb was disappointed. He thought for large parts of the fight Freddie was the better man and should have put London away.

They drove back to Upavon in silence. Freddie felt he had let Ted down. Ted, on the other hand, believed Freddie had not taken the fight seriously and it showed in the latter stages. They did not even speak when Broadribb dropped Freddie back at camp.

The following morning, Freddie was called in to see his commanding officer. He had finally got the news he had been expecting for the past few years. He was to be posted overseas to India. Immediately, he phoned Broadribb to tell him his next fight would be his last.

When Freddie entered the ring to face the Scottish heavyweight Ken Shaw at the Queensbury Club on 10 February 1945, it was to be his last fight in Britain for 15 months. As in the meeting with London, Mills was giving away nearly 3st to his opponent.

The well-dressed crowd, who had paid a premium to see Freddie fight, were shocked to see him walk on to a beautiful right hand to the jaw in the fourth round, dumping him on the seat of his pants for a count of nine. However, the knockdown was the only bright spot for the Scot in an increasingly brutal and bloody affair.

By the seventh, Freddie was back in control. Shaw, who had been on the floor himself in the sixth round, was wearing a mask of blood and the horror show was complete when a punch from Mills split open Shaw's face from his nose down to his lip. Immediately, Mills backed off and the gory affair was brought to an end by the referee. Shaw would be scarred for life and needed six stitches in the wound.

After three months in India, things had not really changed all that much. Freddie had seen no military action. Drilling continued each day. There were a few sporadic exhibitions to boost the morale of the troops but very little to do for the war effort. Once the novelty of being overseas had worn off, Freddie was bothered by the heat and plagued by insects.

Things were made worse by the sub-standard food and there were a few occasions when Freddie was laid low by stomach cramps. He was never in one place for very long, moving through Calcutta and Bombay. Everywhere he went, he was faced with poverty and street peddlers.

It was a welcome relief when the RAF informed him that he was to join up with the army, but would still hold his RAF badges and rank, as part of the Service Sports and Entertainment Control Committee (ISSEC).

Like its equivalent, the Entertainment National Service Association, the primary aim of the ISSEC was to entertain the troops with sporting exhibitions. Freddie's role was to put on a show of his boxing skills and then answer a few questions about his career. His easy manner and warmth made him a big hit with the servicemen.

More importantly, it allowed him to bond with a large group of men that included his old foe Al Robinson and Denis Compton. Like Freddie, Compton, who forged twin sports careers as a footballer for Arsenal in the winter and a cricketer for Middlesex in summer, would go on to make a substantial living by starring in advertisements and endorsements, most notably for the hair product Brylcreem.

Each day, Compton would organise an 11-a-side football match, then Mills would spar with his old foe Robinson during the half-time break. From there, Freddie and Al would travel with the football team as they moved from station to station across the Indian sub-continent.

Freddie's ability to speak in front of large crowds, his sense of humour and mischief-making would serve him well over the next decade as he forged a media career. For most servicemen, their preferred act was a blue comedian or dancing girls, not two men slugging it out. Winning them over was a major achievement.

For Freddie, it was just like being back on the boxing booths. After turning one particularly raucous crowd around, Denis Compton sought out Freddie and said, 'You know, you have a real talent for this. You should give serious consideration to going into showbusiness once you stop fighting.'

Showbusiness may have been a bit of fun when he was entertaining the troops overseas, but boxing remained his livelihood. His time away had had an adverse impact on his finances. Pay had been irregular and the £60 gratuity payment from the RAF was not going to last forever.

When he docked in Liverpool in early 1946 to be demobbed from the RAF, he had only one thing on his mind. He had to get back into the ring and there was only one man who could help him do that, Ted Broadribb.

11

If only…

THE car turned left into Terrace Road, where many familiar faces from the past waved at Freddie as he arrived. The street party had been weeks in the planning. Large tables filled with food were laid along the road, which was closed off especially for the occasion. The war was over and the bunting was out especially to greet Freddie.

It was only supposed to be a small family gathering but Bournemouth wanted to celebrate the achievements of its favourite son with an old-fashioned street party in his honour. Even the mayor was on hand to greet him as Freddie climbed out of Ted Broadribb's car. He posed for photographs then greeted his parents, who waited on their doorstep beaming with pride.

His mother wrapped her arms around her youngest son, smothering him in kisses, while his father, a man of few words at the best of times, reached out to shake Freddie's hand. 'Welcome home, son,' was all the former rag and bone man had to say.

The crowd of family and well-wishers called for a speech from the man they had all come to see. Composing himself, standing in his front doorway, Freddie said, 'I am so happy to be home. Hopefully the next time I come back, I will be able to show off the world championship belt as this morning I have signed to fight Gus Lesnevich.'

The boxing scene had changed beyond all recognition during Freddie's absence. Jack Solomons, the man who had once been so impressed by Freddie and tried to sign him up to a managerial contract, was now the top promoter in Britain.

After developing a relationship with American promoter Mike Jacobs, Solomons was able to bring over the very best talent from the States to fight in the UK. This meant that Freddie could finally find out if he really was the best light-heavyweight champion in the world by facing Gus Lesnevich.

Just before heading down to Bournemouth for the welcome-home party, Freddie signed a contract with Solomons to fight Lesnevich. The paperwork stipulated that Freddie would receive 22.5 per cent of the gross receipts of the gate as his financial reward. Broadribb would get 33.3 per cent of whatever was left over after all expenses were paid.

If anybody suspected Len Harvey and Jock McAvoy were over the hill when they were beaten by Freddie, there was no way the same could be said of Gus Lesnevich.

By the time the former US coastguard signed up to face Mills he had been world champion for five years, winning the title in 1941. His path to the top had been tougher than Freddie's, including facing Billy Conn, a fighter who'd given Joe Louis all sorts of trouble in two fights.

However, Freddie would have taken a lot of encouragement after Lesnevich was knocked out in six rounds by heavyweight Lee Oma in his first fight after being discharged from the service. Freddie would train for his title fight at Solomons' gymnasium in Great Windmill Street, where the promoter also kept a suite of offices.

After the Jack London fight, Ted Broadribb was convinced Freddie lost because he lacked focus in his training. Therefore, he insisted his fighter team up with top coach Nat Seller. With slicked-back hair and horn-rimmed glasses, Seller looked more like a bank manager than a boxing trainer. However, he was Broadribb's go-to man for his stable of fighters. His task in training camp was to ensure Freddie's mind stayed on the job in hand.

His sparring partners were old friend and RAF colleague Duggie Bygrave and former opponent Dave McCleave. Mills arrived for training weighing over 13st 7lb, one stone above the light-heavyweight limit of 12st 7lb. There was a lot of work to be done. Training did not get off to a good start. Freddie complained of feeling tired and sluggish.

Things got worse when Freddie had to leave his training camp altogether after the news came through that his father Tom had been taken seriously ill. Sadly, the welcome party was the last time Freddie would ever see his father alive. He did not make it home in time and his father passed away before he got back to Bournemouth. Freddie was devastated. 'I can't go on, mum. I am going to postpone the fight. I should have been there for him and I wasn't.'

Despite disapproving of his boxing career for much of her life, Lottie urged Freddie to go on. Nothing gave Tom more pride than seeing his son in the ring. After a few days, Freddie returned to camp reinvigorated. He desperately wanted to beat Lesnevich and dedicate the win to his father.

On the afternoon of the fight, Freddie suffered from nerves. This was the biggest bout of his career. All sorts of doubts ran through his mind. Had he done enough? Was he ready for a fight of this magnitude? He had, after all, been out of the ring for 15 months.

At the weigh-in, it became obvious that Freddie's preparations had been far from ideal. He scaled 12st 5lb 14oz, while Lesnevich came in right on the limit of 12st 7lb. Freddie was disappointed. He had lost too much weight too quickly. He always made a point of coming in bang on the limit, even if it meant sitting in a Turkish bath a few hours before fight night. He feared the weight loss would affect his power against the teak-tough American.

Despite weighing lighter than his opponent, from a financial point of view things were looking very good. Deciding to accept 22.5 per cent of the gate receipts looked a masterstroke. As with many of Freddie's wartime fights, Haringey Arena was packed to the rafters, with tickets being exchanged for up to £20 each. As Freddie prepared to make his way to the ring, there were some 15,000 fight fans there to cheer Britain's favourite boxer on to world title glory.

Sat in his dressing room waiting for the buzzer to call him to the ring, Freddie was apprehensive. The usual visit from the British Board of Boxing Control inspectors came and went, and he felt the kind of nerves he had not experienced since the first time he climbed through the ropes as a novice. His legs and arms had felt heavy before he walked out to fight Len Harvey but this time he felt much worse, gripped with tension.

Freddie panicked, worried that he would forget what came so naturally to him. Had he been away too long? Had he prepared right? The press had reported that Lesnevich was in the best shape of his life and was so keen to have the right equipment that he had imported an extra heavy bag from the States so his preparations could be perfect.

The pre-fight meal of steak followed by a glass of champagne, which Freddie had devoured with gusto, weighed heavily on his stomach. Pre-fight wisecracks from Nat Seller as he gave Freddie a final rub-down were just irritating him. All he wanted was silence to concentrate on the matter in hand.

At the appointed time, Freddie put on his dressing gown, with his initials 'FM' emblazoned on his back. The crowd, which was peppered with the celebrities of the day, waited excitedly for the man from Bournemouth, who aimed to become the first British undisputed world champion in 30 years. It was all a far cry from the hospitals and football pitches in India, where he had been putting on exhibitions for the past 18 months.

As Freddie made his way to the ring, even the crowd could not lift him. He felt stiff and tense, as though he was already several rounds into the fight. As he shadow-boxed in the ring, he simply could not shake out the tension from his limbs.

Understandably, Lesnevich started much the quicker of the two, throwing a couple of lefts to head and body as he danced around the ring. A left to the ribs for the unusually cautious Mills resulted in a clinch. Compared to the fast-moving American, Freddie looked slow and cumbersome and the best action in the opening round came from Lesnevich. He managed to snap Freddie's head back with a left to the nose and a right hook to the jaw. There was very little doubt that Lesnevich had taken the first round and Freddie was clearly feeling the effects of his long lay-off.

As he sat on his stool between rounds, he looked out to the vast crowd. The huge arc lights made the ring feel hot. It dawned on him that his hopes of shaking off his ring-rust, and settling his pre-fight nerves with a good first round, had been lost as the bell sounded for the second.

Freddie made a better start to round two, connecting with a left to Lesnevich's midriff. As the former US coastguard moved out of the way, much to the crowd's delight the American tumbled to the canvas. Ruling it a slip, referee Eugene Henderson pulled the two men to the centre of the ring. Once the action restarted, Freddie worked the body with two-fisted aggression but it had little effect and Lesnevich responded by fending off Freddie with clean jabs to the face. That changed the dynamic of the fight and by now Mills was locked in a grim battle for survival.

Showing why he had sat on top of the world for the past five years, Lesnevich delivered a thunderous right cross that exploded on Freddie's jaw. It rocked him back on his heels and Lesnevich, gazelle-like, went after his prey, throwing another brutal right that deposited his opponent on the floor. Freddie, too eager, was up quickly at the count of six.

The storm was not over as the same clinical right hand saw Mills quickly back on the canvas. Again, he got up at the count of six. Lesnevich was in total control and put Freddie down for a count of eight with another right. Mustering all his resilience, Freddie fought against the pain as Lesnevich tore into him again, keen to bring an early end to the fight.

It was not long before Freddie was down for the fourth time, this time for a count of nine. As he stood in the centre of the ring, steeling himself for another onslaught from the American, he looked like a beaten man. The bell rang to save him from further punishment.

For the capacity crowd and those listening on the radio at home, the minute-long interval between the rounds was nothing more than a stay of execution. Freddie was so bamboozled that he could have been back in the Westover Ice Rink for all he knew.

At the end of the second round, he had walked towards the American's corner. Given the beating and four knockdowns during the second session, many must have wondered why the referee didn't step in or why Freddie's corner didn't throw in the towel.

Freddie would never be able to remember what happened from the start of the second round through to the end of the fight. Broadribb simply told his fighter to keep out of the way of Lesnevich's punches – hardly expert advice.

As the bell rang for the third round, the crowd expected Lesnevich to finish it. But Mills, showing few ill effects from the pummelling he had taken in the previous round, began working the body of the New Jersey man.

Lesnevich responded by going to Freddie's body, only to miss with a right. In reply, Mills threw a rod-like left to Lesnevich's face, drawing blood from his nose. In the turbulence of the second round, very few observers had noticed a cut over the left eye of the American. In the third, Mills the brawler demonstrated his boxing skill by throwing some beautifully timed shots to face and body, forcing Lesnevich to miss in the process.

Halfway through the round Freddie had the home crowd on their feet, showing the type of power that had dispatched Len Harvey four years earlier. He smashed away at the head and body of Lesnevich. At the end of the round, Freddie walked back to his corner largely unmarked while the small cut over the eye of Lesnevich had begun to swell. From somewhere, Freddie had found some added resolve.

The fourth started much like the first, with Lesnevich rushing at Freddie. This time he was ready, with a fresh wind, and a straight right hand knocked the American off his stride. Mills then followed this up with some fierce body punching. A huge right from Freddie saw Lesnevich's eye begin to close and the Englishman started to dominate the fight. This was what the crowd had paid to see and they roared their approval. Every time the American tried to attack he was met with a left jab, followed by a strong right hook.

Between rounds, the American's corner worked frantically on his closing left eye. The fourth round was the first he had clearly lost and Freddie, although he couldn't remember it later, must have been very satisfied with his progress.

If the pendulum had begun to swing in Freddie's favour in the fourth round, his confident start to the fifth had most people thinking the fight was slipping away from Lesnevich. Targeting the damaged eye with accurate left hands, Freddie mixed those punches with shots to the body. Nothing Lesnevich tried seemed to work as Mills moved in and out of range, ending the round strongly with a couple of flashing right hands to Lesnevich's head.

It was clear that Freddie had recovered from the early onslaught. It almost seemed as though Lesnevich was facing a different fighter as Mills used his jab to control the action while keeping his opponent out of range. This was a new side to Freddie's boxing, one the British public had never seen before.

Not learning his lesson from the previous round, Lesnevich again rushed at Mills at the start of the sixth. The response was much the same, the only change being that Mills tied

109

up Lesnevich as he attacked. Lesnevich had become badly handicapped by his closing left eye but he still showed flashes of brilliance. Two good right hooks from Freddie had the crowd on their feet as the American was left rocked.

During the interval, panic befell the American's corner. They were unable to stop the swelling over the left eye and by then also had a broken nose to contend with. Their efforts were to little avail. As Lesnevich stood to answer the bell for the seventh round, he was practically blind in his left eye and breathing heavily through his mouth.

Despite his restrictions, Lesnevich was still boxing strongly but Freddie, who since the second round had appeared to slow down and time his punches better, shrugged off each attack. The seventh saw the action see-saw between the fighters but Lesnevich's face showed the effects of a hard fight.

In the rest minute, the American's corner again went to work on the swollen eye but it had little effect and Lesnevich changed tack, opting for a lateral movement around Mills. It didn't help him as Freddie, firmly on top, meted out more punishment on the American. Despite the heavy blows, Lesnevich's legs did not buckle. Throughout the round, Freddie continued to build up a points lead.

In comparison to the frantic efforts to ensure Lesnevich answered the bell for the start of each round, Freddie's corner was calm after the drama of the second. Broadribb told Mills he was ahead on points and certainly at this stage he was in control.

As the fight wore on Lesnevich, hindered by his injuries, began to tire but Freddie appeared fresher with each round. The ninth followed the pattern of the bout, with Lesnevich walking on to a straight left followed by a right hook. The

American's face was a mess but Freddie's punches did not seem to affect his legs. The brave Lesnevich was trailing but he was still in it, and any time Freddie eased off the gas he went looking for the Briton with attacks of his own.

In an after-dinner speech a long time after the fight, Freddie would say that he remembered little, if anything, of the fight from rounds two to nine and fought them on instinct alone, such was the fog in which he had been left after his disastrous start. During the minute's rest after the ninth, Freddie's head cleared. Ignoring Broadribb's advice that he was ahead on points and just had to stick it out, Freddie decided to go for broke and charge straight at Lesnevich in an effort to end the bout.

Instead, a desperate Lesnevich came at Freddie but was met with a flurry of heavy blows to the body. A solid right cross from Lesnevich was answered by a strong right followed by a left hand, which had brought Freddie so much success.

Halfway through the round, Lesnevich's bravery and aggression would eventually tell as, for the first time since the second round, Freddie took a backward step. A strong shot to the body brought down the guard of the retreating Briton and suddenly Lesnevich sensed an opening. He was too good a champion not to press home the advantage.

A left cross landed perfectly on Freddie's jaw followed by a massive overhand right then a huge uppercut. It was this shot that put Freddie on his knees for a count of eight. After tasting blood, and with his left eye closed, Lesnevich went in for the kill and three right hands in quick succession sent Freddie to the floor for the second time.

Just as he had in the second round, Freddie forgot to take the count on one knee and got up at four. After failing to press home his early advantage, there was no way the world champion was going to let Freddie off the hook this time. On rubber legs with his senses scrambled, his opponent was a sitting duck. Seeing that Mills was in no condition to defend himself any longer, Lesnevich did not really want to hit his opponent any more. However, he was a fighting man with a job to do, so he rushed across the ring and sent Freddie back to the canvas with an exquisite right hand.

Freddie desperately tried to use the ropes to haul himself back to his feet. The attempt was futile as referee Eugene Henderson had seen more than enough and called the fight off after reaching a count of three. Only four seconds remained of the round and it was Lesnevich who could now lay claim to being the undisputed light-heavyweight champion of the world.

As Freddie was shown to his corner, he was still unaware of what had happened, unaware that he had lost the fight. Freddie did not know what day of the week it was. 'I'm all right, I'm all right,' he kept repeating over and over again.

There was a tap on the dressing room door. Having been told of the British tradition that the winner visits the loser after the fight, Lesnevich called in on Freddie and his team to see how he was.

What Lesnevich found shocked him. Freddie was lying prostrate on a rub-down table, with the room in virtual darkness. Ted Broadribb explained that Freddie had complained the light was hurting his eyes. Freddie was not moving or even making a sound.

For a few seconds, Lesnevich thought Freddie was dead. 'How ya doing, Freddie? That was one hell of a fight you put up in there.' The champion greeted his opponent by extending his arm for a handshake.

There was still no reply or movement from the beaten fighter. 'Freddie, Freddie, it's Gus Lesnevich. He's come to see how you are,' Broadribb told him.

Still, there was no response. 'Come into the light so he can get a better look at you,' Broadribb told Lesnevich.

Eventually Freddie, who was still lying flat on his back, turned his head to face the champion. He did not say a word, failing to acknowledge the presence of the man who had shared the ring with him just 20 minutes earlier.

'Give it an hour or so and he'll be fine. He's always like this after a fight,' Broadribb said.

As he left the dressing room, Lesnevich turned to his trainer. 'I should never have thrown that punch. The referee should have stopped it – he was helpless. Now look at him.'

For over an hour, Freddie lay there on the table without moving. It was only when Jack Solomons came into the room to tell Broadribb they were both needed for a press conference that the manager, with the help of Nat Seller, got Freddie changed.

At the press conference after the fight, Freddie still couldn't say a word. Dazed and confused, Broadribb answered questions on his behalf. 'It has been a tough fight but Freddie will be back in three weeks against Bruce Woodcock,' he said. There would be a few days' rest but Freddie would return to full training in a matter of days, Broadribb told the journalists.

On the way home, Broadribb had to stop his car several times as Freddie began to come round, only to complain of feeling nauseous. He vomited at the side of the road.

The effects of the fight did not subside for weeks. Freddie was left punch-drunk and incoherent. When he did talk, his speech was slurred. Each morning, he had to be awakened from a deep sleep. It was so bad that Freddie thought he was in a coma. Watching the fight years later, Mills was unequivocal in his verdict. He said that no boxer could take the type of punishment he took in the ring that night and expect to be the same person afterwards.

The sporting press called the fight the 'battle of thrills' but were hugely critical of referee Henderson for stopping the action before reaching the mandatory count of ten. As the bout was called off with only four seconds left in the round, many felt that with Freddie ahead on the scorecards after the amazing recovery he had staged, he would have recovered to win the fight after another minute's rest.

The patriotic media were clutching at straws. Lesnevich had beaten Freddie into submission and Broadribb felt that Henderson had made the right call. So too did both fighters. The only real hope Freddie had of winning had he survived the tenth round was Lesnevich being retired by his corner because of his swollen eye and broken nose. Henderson retired from refereeing in the aftermath of the fight but Freddie had no complaint with the official.

It was after this bout that Freddie's blinding headaches became more frequent and they would blight the rest of his life. What was clear even though Freddie had lost, his performance had been valiant. The way he fought his way back into the fight after the disastrous second round meant there were still big nights ahead for Mills. Fearless Freddie was not finished yet.

12

Trouble at the Den

THE posters and tickets had been printed. Flyers for Freddie's next fight were already being handed out even before he had entered the ring to face Gus Lesnevich. In little over three weeks' time, Freddie would face British heavyweight champion Bruce Woodcock in a non-title bout.

A fight against Woodcock made perfect sense. A win for Freddie would show he could mix it with the heavyweights, opening the door to a potential clash with Joe Louis. Woodcock had knocked out nearly all of his opponents and developed a massive following among British fight fans. A huge gate would be guaranteed.

'Well, Freddie, what are we going to do about the Woodcock fight?' Broadribb asked him a few mornings after Lesnevich.

The last thing Freddie wanted to do was climb through the ropes but he was not going to tell Broadribb that. 'I don't know, I really don't, Ted.' Secretly, he hoped his manager would pull him out.

'Well, I don't want to put any pressure on but tickets have been sold. Jack Solomons tells me the contract is so tight you would have to pay compensation. It could cost you.'

Having been convinced any symptoms he was suffering from would soon pass, a despondent Freddie made his way to The Den, Millwall Football Club's ground to begin training.

It was almost impossible to work out in the first few days. He was too sore to begin roadwork and the headaches impeded his ability to spar. The only physical activity he undertook in the first week was an impromptu kickabout with the Millwall lads and some labouring on the new stand being built there.

When sparring with Duggie Bygrave finally begun, something was wrong with Freddie. He was heavily knocked to the floor by a soft-looking right hook from Bygrave and it was the third time he hit the deck in one session. The first time, Freddie told Nat Seller it was a slip. The second, he had simply been knocked off balance. But this was a real knockdown. Had it been a real fight, the referee would have begun the count.

The most worrying thing was that Freddie made no attempt to get up. He just lay there, exhausted.

'Come on, Freddie, get up.' Seller implored.

'Quit playing around, get up, Freddie,' Duggie Bygrave urged.

'Why don't you two just fuck off? You're working me into the ground,' an angry Freddie shouted at the two men. Neither had seen Freddie lose his temper like this before.

There had been subtle changes to Freddie's demeanour in this training camp. He had always been happy go lucky but was now easily angered. Duggie had noticed it a few days earlier in a friendly football match with the Millwall lads.

One of the boys tackled Freddie late, taking his legs from under him. Rather than laughing it off, Freddie jumped up, grabbed the lad by the shirt and threatened to smash his face in. It was only the intervention of Duggie and a few others that calmed Freddie down.

'Let's just back off for a few days, shall we, Nat?' Duggie suggested to Seller as Freddie headed off to the showers. The rest of the training camp mainly consisted of Freddie running lap after lap around the perimeter of the football ground.

'There is no way he will be ready for Woodcock, Ted. Running is no substitute for sparring. He's not been in the ring for over a week now.' Nat Seller reported back to Broadribb, who rang to ask how Freddie was getting on.

Despite the smiles and the handshakes at the weigh-in, Freddie was seething. 'How's it looking, Freddie?' Ted asked as his fighter stepped off the scales. Freddie had come in at 12st 13lb, eight pounds heavier than when weighing in ahead of his fight against Lesnevich but a full ten pounds lighter than the much bigger Woodcock, who came in at 13st 9lb.

'You heard, he's ten pounds heavier than me. He's walked through everyone and you stuck me in with him, three weeks after Lesnevich knocked seven bells out of me.'

The atmosphere in the dressing room was no different to the training camp. The mood was dark and heavy. When Freddie had waited to face Lesnevich, he was almost paralysed with nerves, his arms and legs heavy, such was the anticipation. Things were markedly different this time. Still suffering with blinding headaches, he was not relishing being hit by the hard punches of the bigger man.

Despite defeat against Lesnevich, Freddie remained the hottest property in British boxing. If his name appeared on a boxing bill, promoters were guaranteed a sell-out.

The capacity crowd at the Harringay Arena expected a drawn-out battle between two of Britain's most exciting fighters. For Freddie, it was a completely different story as he made the walk to the ring. He felt like a man who was about to take his final walk to the gallows.

Freddie's star had not faded as he climbed through the ropes to huge cheers, but it was a similar story to the build-up to the Lesnevich fight. He couldn't shake out the stiffness in his arms and legs. Ever since he left the ring after Lesnevich, there had been a constant pain in his head. Tonight, a headache was developing into a migraine, made worse by the bright ring lights.

As the referee brought Mills and Woodcock together for their final instructions, Freddie was squinting at his opponent, struggling to focus on him. 'Do not go toe to toe with this boy,' Broadribb told his fighter before the bell sounded for the first round.

Even if he wanted to, Freddie was in no position to come out on the front foot and try and rush his taller, heavier opponent. Woodcock was nowhere as near as fast as Lesnevich but he was a wily boxer who showed good skill in the opening round. He threw straight lefts that caught Mills flush on the chin and hurt Freddie with a few rights to the jaw. The majority of the judges' scorecards at ringside showed Woodcock had taken the first round, but despite his obvious discomfort Freddie felt he had given a good account of himself.

With the memory of the second round with Lesnevich still fresh in his mind, Freddie came out of his corner cautiously, staying out of range using his left. Every time Freddie got in range, he was punished by Woodcock. By the end of the round, Freddie's eye was beginning to swell.

Even at this early stage, as he sat on his stool between the second and third rounds, Freddie was already breathing heavily through his mouth. Woodcock's punches were beginning to tell, Freddie's head was pounding and he was already fatigued.

Feeling as though he would not last the distance, Mills decided to throw caution to the wind and go for it in round three. Looking to use his quicker hands and footwork to his advantage, Freddie began moving out of the way of Woodcock's right hands, making the bigger man look clumsy when he swung wildly. Freddie finally found his feet, managing to inflict some damage with two vicious right hooks, with a huge red welt developing under Woodcock's eye just before the bell.

Still, as Freddie sat on the stool for the break, he knew things were not right. Feeling sick, his head throbbing, he told Broadribb there was nothing left in the tank. 'Cut the gloves off, Ted, I've had enough.'

'Shut up Fred, you're on top. He's slow and you are catching him. Keep up the good work,' Broadribb urged as he pushed his man out for the fourth round.

The fourth began badly for Freddie. Two huge left hands from Woodcock hurt him early on. Things then went from bad to worse as a glancing right caught him on the top of his head, sending him to his knees. Mills made the all-too-familiar mistake and was up on his feet too soon. Now his left eye was beginning to close.

When he sat down at the end of the round, Broadribb asked him how he was feeling. 'I can't take any of his punches,' Freddie answered. 'Everything hurts, you're going to have to stop it, Ted.'

Again, Broadribb ignored him. 'Sip on this, it will give you a boost,' Broadribb advised as he pushed a bottle of champagne to Freddie's lips before pouring the rest over his fighter's head.

'Remember to move your head as he is coming in,' Ted shouted as Freddie rose ready for the fifth round.

Ringside observers agreed there was a marked improvement in Freddie's work in the following round. Freddie circled around the slower champion, using his left hand to good effect to inflict even more damage on Woodcock's left eye. Freddie knew he had his man hurt as Woodcock began dabbing at his eye with his glove.

The end of the round, which had been Freddie's best of the fight, saw blood flowing from Woodcock's nose. 'Go in for the kill, you got him, Fred,' Broadribb implored. Freddie said nothing. He was so tired and it was an effort just to get off the stool for the next round.

What Freddie and Broadribb did not know was that Woodcock's corner was getting extremely concerned about the damage to their fighter's left eye. Despite their best efforts, they could not get the swelling down. As the bell rang for the sixth, Woodcock's manager Tommy Hurst told the Doncaster man he needed to go for a knockout before the eye got any worse.

Heeding the warning from Hurst, Woodcock came out for the sixth round determined to be on the front foot. There was no way Woodcock would allow damage to his eye to force an early stoppage. Woodcock caught the incoming Freddie with two huge rights that made the smaller man's legs buckle. With the crowd on their feet, the man they called Fearless Freddie came roaring back, evening up the round on the judge's scorecards.

Between the sixth and seventh rounds, it was the turn of Freddie's corner to work frantically on their fighter's own damaged left eye. But like Woodcock's corner, they found nothing worked and Freddie entered the next round almost entirely reliant on one eye. Luckily for Freddie, Woodcock had the same problem and was throwing desperate right hands hoping one would connect on the jaw of his gallant foe.

If Woodcock had had the speed of Lesnevich, Freddie would have been in serious trouble. But his slower opponent and lack of vision meant Freddie could evade punishment, and when Woodcock did connect he failed to press home his advantage. Nonetheless, Freddie was still on the wrong end of some fierce blows in the eighth.

Ahead of the ninth round, Freddie's corner told him to 'stay out of trouble'. At that stage, a tiring Freddie was beginning to cover up. That didn't stop a huge left greeting Freddie as he charged in. After a bad opening, he began using his left hand more effectively, catching Woodcock with a good right cross, before the bigger man responded with some solid defensive work. It was only Freddie's bravery that was carrying him through the fight.

The tenth round opened with some good boxing from both fighters. Freddie took a right hook to the jaw and his legs temporarily bent. When two more rights landed Woodcock moved in looking to end the fight before the scheduled 12 rounds. But Freddie shook off any ill effects to fire back with some bombs of his own, pushing Woodcock against the ropes.

The crowd were on the edge of their seats and both men were desperate at this stage of the fight as every round seemed to take a huge amount of energy out of them. Freddie's face was badly swollen, as was Woodcock's.

Come the 11th round both boxers, looking tired and hurt, threw caution to the wind in a bid to end the contest.

Ferociously trading blows in a real seesaw battle, both men went looking for the punch to finish the fight, but neither found it.

It was a testament to Freddie's fortitude that he even made it out for the 12th round. He had taken everything Woodcock could throw at him and was somehow still standing. After Freddie took a sip of a freshly opened bottle of champagne, Broadribb threw the rest over the body of his fighter and whispered in his ear, 'Take this round and we will be drinking this stuff for the next month.'

Biting down hard on his mouth guard, Freddie was determined to knock Woodcock out. As the referee pulled both fighters together to touch gloves for the 12th and final round, Freddie stared intently at his man.

As the bell rang, Freddie was as good as his word, going toe to toe with Woodcock. After catching the Doncaster fighter with a right to his damaged eye, Woodcock responded with a right of his own to Freddie's head. The pair traded heavy punches for much of the round before the final bell finally separated them.

Shortly after the final bell rang, Woodcock's hand was raised in victory. Not that Freddie was aware. It was not until his return to the dressing room that he was told he had lost the fight. It seemed Freddie had blacked out after the eighth round and could not remember anything.

'It's time for a holiday, Freddie. How does a couple of days in America grab you?' Broadribb smiled at Freddie a few days after the Woodcock fight.

Freddie thought it was a great idea. He had not really had a rest since he returned from India. His time had been taken up by fighting and training. The trip was made all the more attractive when Broadribb informed him that he also had tickets for the rematch between Joe Louis and Billy Conn.

Both Broadribb and Solomons, who would also undertake the trip, hoped to line up some American opposition for Freddie. It did not happen. An enjoyable couple of days in the Big Apple ended with Freddie providing some expert analysis of the fight for BBC Radio.

'I want you to meet Johnny Nilsson, Freddie,' Broadribb said to his fighter on the night of the Louis-Conn fight. He did not know it at the time but he was shaking hands with his next opponent.

The fight against the Swede was made for 13 August and would be fought at the Withdean Stadium in Brighton. The bout would be a heavyweight contest. 'He's not in Woodcock's league, the guy is nothing more than a novice,' Broadribb reassured Freddie, who was reluctant about stepping in with the big men again.

It was only Nilsson's tenth professional fight in a career that had already seen him lose one and draw another. It was also the first and only time he had fought outside his native Sweden.

On his return to the UK, Freddie headed to Brighton and began the long hours of sparring and roadwork around Preston Park, to the north of the then-bustling seaside resort. On paper, the fight with Nilsson would be a good way of rebuilding confidence after successive poundings at the hands of Lesnevich and Woodcock – and so it proved.

It was a relatively straightforward affair. Looking to ease himself into the fight, Freddie came out for the first round feeling out his man with few left jabs. A right cross followed by a left uppercut rocked the Swede, bringing a roar from the crowd.

Even at this early stage, it was clear Freddie was in a different class to his much heavier opponent. Freddie quickly set about his work, opening up with both hands, and a big left to the jaw sent Nilsson to the floor. The Swede rose at the count of six but it was only a matter of time before Freddie finished him off.

Freddie rarely missed an opportunity to end a bout with an opponent hurt, and it wasn't long before Nilsson was back on the deck, again for a count of six. Knowing the fight had gone from the Swede, Freddie finished him with a flurry of punches that ended with a hard right to the jaw, which sent his opponent under the ropes and on to the ring apron. Despite Nilsson's best efforts to crawl back into the ring, the referee had seen enough and the contest was waved over before the end of the first round.

Lifting his hands as the referee waved the fight over, Freddie acknowledged the crowd, who had chanted 'Freddie! Freddie! Freddie!' from the moment he began his walk to the ring. However, there was one problem that loomed large on the horizon – money.

After taking home huge purses from his fights with Lesnevich and Woodcock, Freddie was still short of cash. Having received a small cheque, which came to only a tenth of what was taken on the gate for both fights, Freddie went around to see Broadribb. 'When am I going to see the money for the Lesnevich and Woodcock fights, Ted?'

'You've already been paid, Freddie.'

'I know that but when does the rest of the money come through?'

There was no more money. After taxes, payments to Nat Seller and sparring partners and a managerial fee to Broadribb, the cheque of £500 was all that was left of the huge contracts Freddie had signed for the two biggest fights of his career.

Freddie was incredulous. He had fought in some of the biggest fights Britain had seen for years but had nothing to show for it. He asked how he could make more money. The answer from Ted Broadribb was simple: he had to get bigger. The money was in the heavyweights.

Advising Freddie to take August and September off, Broadribb told Freddie of an American fighter, Joe Baksi, who was due to tour Britain at the end of the year. He was a real contender for Joe Louis' crown. Anyone who beat him would have the opportunity to face the world heavyweight champion.

Both Jack Solomons and Ted Broadribb were keen for Freddie to get the first crack at the American. Freddie liked the idea. The world heavyweight championship was the richest prize in sport and would set him up for life. That summer, he dreamed of facing off against Louis. First, though, he had to get past Baksi, which would be much more difficult than he could ever imagine.

13

You'll think
of something

SO far, they had found four cuts around the eyes but the blood would not stop flowing. 'Close your eyes, Mr Mills, there is something we are missing.' Finally, the King's College doctor found the fifth and final cut between Freddie's eyelashes.

There was not a single part of Freddie's body that did not hurt. Joe Baksi had hit him from every angle. The doctor was so concerned about the beating Freddie had taken that he wanted to admit him for observation overnight. Despite struggling to see from cuts under his eyes, ever the hard man, Freddie elected to go back to Ted's house instead.

It had all started so well. Back once again in Brighton training with former opponent Dave McCleave and the ever-present Duggie Bygrave providing the sparring, Freddie felt fit and healthy, and was looking forward to the challenge big Joe Baksi presented.

Having been told that the former miner from Pennsylvania was a fearsome body puncher who did his best work on the inside, Nat Seller instructed both sparring partners to rough

Freddie up a bit in anticipation of Baksi's 'take no prisoners' style of fighting.

Upon the announcement of the fight, the press were scathing. Labelling the bout as a total mismatch, they predicted Baksi would be too much for Mills, too tall and way too heavy for Freddie to have any chance. They said if Freddie lasted the full 15 rounds, he could count himself lucky.

In an effort to increase Freddie's strength, Nat Seller prescribed a daily pint of Guinness. It was while supping on the drink that Nat first told Freddie about an idea he had. 'How about we bring in a wrestler to put you through your paces? He will throw you around a bit. That way, you can get used to Baksi's tactics.'

A bemused Freddie could not see how it would help him but was willing to give it a try. So the next day, Mo Kikki, a wrestler friend of Seller and Broadribb, was holding Freddie in a headlock. It was then that Freddie felt something pop in his neck.

A rub-down from a masseur the following day did nothing to ease the pain. By the end of the week, Freddie felt numb from the base of his skull right down to the small of his back. Once Freddie felt well enough, he decided to go through light sparring with Duggie Bygrave. It was a disaster. Every punch made him feel dizzy and sick.

The fight with Baksi was only a fortnight away and Freddie was in such pain that he could not even lift up his arms to shadow box in front of the mirror. 'You are going to have to get Ted down here,' Freddie told Seller.

Within hours of receiving the call, Ted Broadribb was at the camp. He came prepared with a manipulator recommended by Jack Solomons. Soon, Freddie was stripped to the waist on the rub-down table as the man worked his magic on his back. After an hour, Freddie was back up and feeling much better.

Eventually, Ted stayed for a few days and was impressed by what he saw. Freddie was like a new man. Even though both Bygrave and McCleave were given instructions to pound on Freddie's body, he was just too fast for them. When they got him in a clinch, he was strong enough to push them off.

Standing on the ring apron with Nat Seller, Ted Broadribb watched the action with a big smile on his face. 'See that, Ted? They are faster than Baksi will ever be and he's making fools of them.' Despite what the press had to say about the fight, based on the evidence of the past few days Broadribb was convinced Freddie was going to pull off a shock.

On the morning of the fight, Broadribb got Freddie to the Harringay Arena extra early for the scheduled weigh-in. The last ten days were some of the best Freddie had ever experienced during a training camp. He felt fit and ready for anything.

'Christ, Ted, that's not him, is it?' Freddie asked his manager as a huge man made his way through the crowd of journalists to join Freddie on the makeshift stage where the weighing scales had been placed for the press and photographers.

'You must be Freddie. I'm Joe,' the visitor said. Freddie shook hands with the man who in a few hours he would be sharing the ring with. His handshake was firm. If Freddie thought Bruce Woodcock was a big man, then Baksi resembled a grizzly bear. He had only ever seen pictures of the former miner from Pennsylvania before. In the flesh, he looked huge.

The weighing scales underlined this. Baksi stripped off his street clothes to reveal a rippling torso. He weighed in at just over 15 stones. The pints of Guinness may have helped Freddie

Freddie ready to take on all comers at Sam McKeowen's boxing booth. The two men rarely saw eye to eye.

Freddie at Chipperfield's travelling fairground with two bullish friends.

Sitting in the middle between Freddie and another booth fighter, Alf Cozens, is Bob Turner, Freddie's first manager who guided him from small shows in Bournemouth to the fringes of the British title.

Freddie began his boxing apprenticeship on the boxing booths of Chipperfield's travelling fairgrounds alongside a number of circus acts.

Jack Solomons, the biggest promoter in British boxing after the war.

Freddie working on his mid-section in preparation for his meeting with British and Empire light-heavyweight champion, Len Harvey.

Ted Broadribb, Freddie's father-in-law and manager. Broadribb would take him to the world title.

A star is born. Freddie swings at champion Len Harvey at Tottenham's White Hart Lane in 1942. The win over Harvey made Freddie the biggest star in British boxing.

Len Harvey's ring craft was no match for Freddie's two-fisted aggression. Harvey found himself knocked through the ropes after two rounds.

'You should have seen the other fella!' Freddie shaking hands with Gus Lesnevich after falling short in his first world title challenge in 1946.

Freddie down against Bruce Woodcock. He would face the popular northern heavyweight twice, coming up short on both occasions.

Joe Baksi was just too big for Freddie. The former coal miner from Pennsylvania dominated their bout from the start before scoring a sixth round win in 1946.

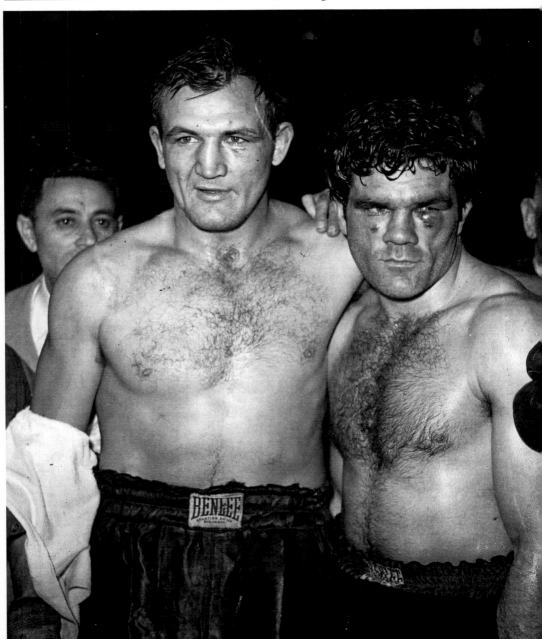

The fight with Lloyd Marshall almost put paid to Freddie's world title ambitions as well as his career after he suffered a broken orbital bone at the hands of the slick American.

Nat Seller looked more like a bank manager than boxing trainer. Here he is celebrating Freddie's world title win with manager, Ted Broadribb.

Freddie in training for the Maxim fight. All had not been well in the camp beforehand.

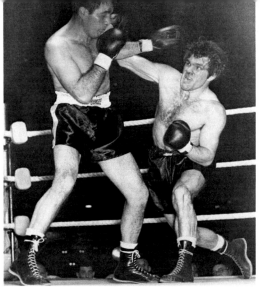

In the early stages against Joey Maxim, Freddie was firmly on top before being stopped in the tenth round. It was his last appearance in a boxing ring.

On top of the world. Joey Maxim after pummelling Freddie into submission in the tenth round of the match-up at Earls Court in 1950.

Freddie on his wedding day with his wife Chrissie in the garden of their home, Joggi Villa. She was Ted Broadribb's daughter, a divorcee and was Freddie's only known girlfriend.

Freddie with his stepson, Don McCorkindale Jr. A family man, Freddie doted on his three children.

After hanging up his gloves, Freddie became a well-known media personality. Here he poses in a publicity still with fellow Six-Five Special presenters, Pete Murray and Josephine Douglas.

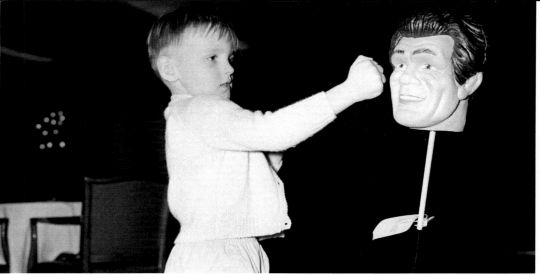

Such was Freddie's fame he would lend his likeness to all sorts of products. Here a young boy tries to land a punch on a Freddie Mills punch ball.

'He couldn't box his way out of a paper bag!' With his great friend Eamonn Andrews, who was to surprise him with the big red book in 1961.

As boxing mad youngsters, Ronnie and Reggie Kray idolised Freddie and would queue up with others to watch him train. Years later they would be regular visitors to his restaurant and nightclub.

The end of a hero. Freddie was pronounced dead on arrival at Middlesex Hospital in the early hours of 25 July 1965.

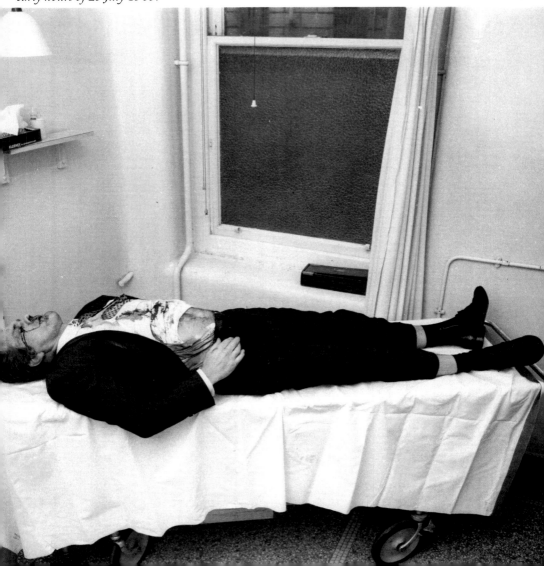

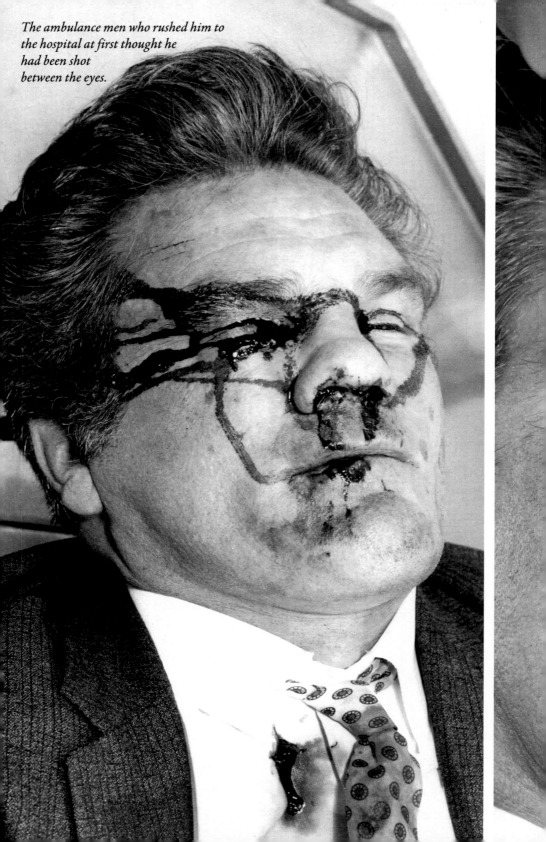

The ambulance men who rushed him to the hospital at first thought he had been shot between the eyes.

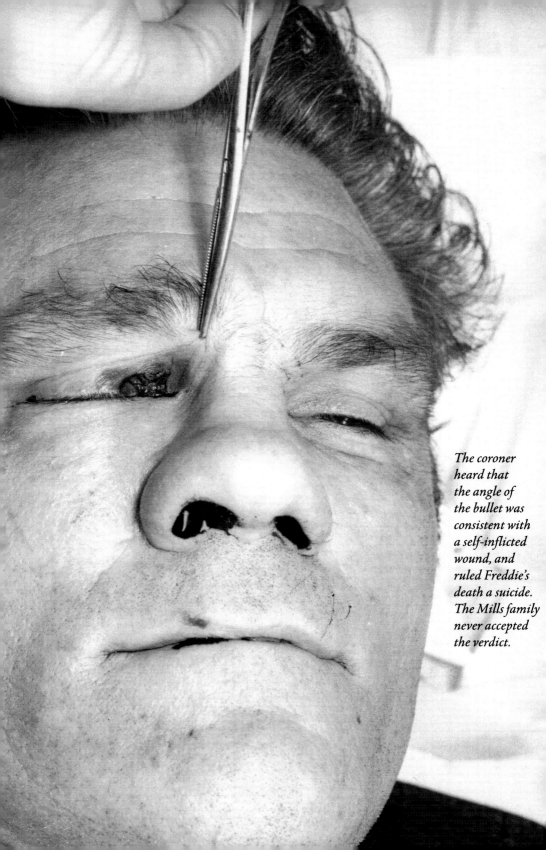

The coroner heard that the angle of the bullet was consistent with a self-inflicted wound, and ruled Freddie's death a suicide. The Mills family never accepted the verdict.

Two worlds come together to mourn Freddie. Entertainer Bruce Forsyth and boxer Henry Cooper at his funeral in Camberwell on 30 July 1965.

Freddie lies at Camberwell New Cemetery. Over 50 years after his death there are still some who will not let him rest in peace.

to bulk up to a career-high 13st 2lbs, but it still meant he gave away 27 pounds in weight to the American. Added to that, Baksi's reach was substantially longer than Freddie's and at 6ft 1in he practically towered over his opponent.

As they stood shaking hands at the conclusion of the weigh-in, Freddie quipped, 'Anyone got a step ladder so at least I can look this fella in the eye?' The assembled journalists laughed but no one gave Freddie any chance of beating the big American.

Later that night at the Harringay Arena, once the national anthems of both countries had been played, both fighters took off their dressing gowns ready for business. Anyone watching could clearly see that Joe Baksi was a fully-fledged heavyweight. Perhaps it was Freddie's mind playing tricks on him but Baksi actually looked bigger in the ring than he did at the weigh-in earlier in the day.

As Nat Seller massaged Freddie's shoulders in an effort to loosen him up before the first bell, he whispered to his fighter, 'Go after him, rush him, he's expecting you to be afraid of him. Show him who's boss around here.'

It was Bonfire Night and Freddie was determined to give the crowd some fireworks. As soon as the bell went for the first round, Freddie ran across the ring and threw a huge left hook that connected with Baksi's jaw. A second left and the audience were roaring Freddie on. Shocked by Freddie's quick start, the American grabbed hold of his much smaller opponent, bearing down on his back with all his weight.

Once the referee told them to break, Freddie again waded in with a right hook that found the spot. A wild left from Freddie gave Baksi the opportunity to go inside, where he launched a ferocious left uppercut that rocked Freddie back on his heels. A straight right that caught Freddie square in the forehead set off the pain in his neck. Another clinch at the end of the round saw the pain spread between Freddie's shoulder blades.

Ignoring the pain, Freddie worked his way on the inside. A heavy left hook to Baksi's body was met with a painful-looking short right to Mills' head. A good hook to the jaw from Freddie gave his corner hope as the bell rang to signal the end of the round.

Freddie was not happy. The pain was intense and he found sitting on the stool uncomfortable, such were the shooting pains down his back. 'Nat, I am in agony, I can't go on.'

Totally ignoring his fighter, Nat told Freddie he had done well in the first round and had hurt the American. Sending Freddie out for the second, he implored him to throw more hooks at Baksi.

In the second round, Baksi showed why he was knocking on the door of a shot at the world heavyweight crown. He was just too good for Freddie and went about his work in a ruthless fashion. Another wicked left uppercut hurt Freddie early in the round and midway through blood began to pour from a cut under his eye.

Trying to fight his way back into the round, Freddie launched a two-fisted body attack. It got him nowhere. Another uppercut, this time from Baksi's right hand, knocked Freddie senseless.

Effective short right hands from the American were too much for Freddie when he came in on the inside. Changing tack, for the rest of the second he tried to box at distance in an effort to keep away from the big American's hurtful punches, but it was futile. Baksi ended the round fully in control with a few short rights to Freddie's jaw. In the corner, Seller and Broadribb worked hard to stem the flow of blood.

'Give me the bucket, I'm going to throw up. Every punch is making me dizzy,' said Freddie. Both Seller and Broadribb again ignored Freddie and simply went about getting their man ready for the next round.

Despite the efforts of his corner, it wasn't long into the third before blood was again streaming from the cut under Freddie's eye. Three straight left hands snapped his head back. A good left hook from Freddie caused Baksi to respond with a series of heavy, short punches. The result saw blood stream from cuts under both of Freddie's eyes. Baksi was clinical in his work, picking his punches and looking to inflict further damage to the eyes. Freddie kept throwing punches but each swing looked more and more desperate.

By now, Freddie complained to his corner of double vision. 'It's like I am fighting two people out there. I don't know where the punches are coming from.'

'Just try and hit both of them!' Nat said. Freddie never knew whether Nat was joking or not.

The fourth round saw Freddie begin more positively but apart from some early success the round followed the same pattern as the rest of the fight. The round opened with a few wild swings from Freddie. A huge right-hand haymaker caught Baksi around the back of the ear but it had absolutely no effect.

The American's short punches were becoming more spiteful. Each shot was more hurtful than the last. A brilliant left hook from Freddie saw Baksi reply with two rights, the first of which caught Mills square on the nose and the second flush on the jaw. There was no way anyone could accuse Freddie of not being busy but the American was soaking up everything Mills was throwing at him.

By the end of the round, it seemed as though Freddie had run out of ideas.

'He's beating me hands down, Ted, there is nothing I can do. I can't hurt him.'

'Don't worry, Freddie, you'll think of something,' replied Ted. Years later, this quip would form the basis of one of Freddie's favourite stories whenever he was called on to give an after-dinner speech.

By the fifth round, Baksi was super confident, throwing short rights to Freddie's face. Looking to give the American something to think about, Freddie threw a few big left hook but it was not long before Baksi got the measure of his opponent, reverting to throwing the short right that was causing Freddie so much trouble.

By the middle of the round, a desperate Freddie reverted to holding on to his opponent, just to catch his breath. After the referee told them to break, Baksi faced Freddie with both hands down by his sides, goading him to land a punch. The crowd at the Harringay Arena, who had little to cheer on the night, began loudly booing and jeering the overseas fighter.

By now, fully settled into his role as the pantomime villain, Baksi lifted his hands in the air at the end of the round as though he had already won the fight. Not that Freddie would have been able to see Baksi's antics. Both eyes were so swollen and puffy that it affected his vision and he could no longer see the heavy punches coming.

It was only a matter of time before the referee would call a halt to the carnage. That didn't worry Broadribb. He urged Mills to go forward for one more valiant effort.

At the start of the sixth, Baksi stopped Mills dead in his tracks with a solid left hand as the referee watched Freddie closely. He was walking on to shots and the only offense he offered were some wild punches that he desperately hoped would connect with Baksi's chin. It was futile. On the odd occasion Freddie did land a punch, it was almost impossible to hurt the big American.

Walking to his corner at the end of the round, Freddie had suffered enough. Dabbing at the cuts under his eyes, he turned to Broadribb and said, 'I'm going to turn it in.'

'Come on, Freddie.'

'No, call the ref over, I've had enough. I could go blind if I carry on. I want out!'

The referee came over, told Broadribb there was no way he was stopping the fight and said he would have to officially retire before wandering over to the neutral corner. After asking Freddie if he was sure he wanted to retire, Broadribb called the referee over again and told him his fighter was retiring because of the cuts under his eyes.

As Baksi walked around the ring triumphant with his hands in the air, the crowd showed their displeasure at the result by throwing rubbish at the American, who simply grinned and carried on strutting around the ring.

Six months later, Baksi faced Freddie's former opponent, the hugely popular Bruce Woodcock. Once again, Baksi would break British hearts, knocking Woodcock down seven times before shattering his jaw and stopping him inside seven rounds. At least Freddie found solace in the fact that Baksi had never managed to knock him off his feet. Joe Baksi would never fight for the world heavyweight championship. He lost a world title eliminator to Ezzard Charles before fading into obscurity.

After the result was announced, Freddie did not hang around. He quickly left the arena to be rushed to hospital. Three days after being sent home from the hospital with 20 stitches to close the cuts to his face, Freddie saw his GP. He had not kept any food down for days, could not sleep because of the crippling neck pain and was so low he wanted to run away.

The doctor told Freddie he was suffering from the after effects of the fight and it would pass in a few days. The neck pain was probably a trapped nerve, the nausea a stomach bug and the depression was put down to exhaustion. There was nothing that could not be fixed without a few days' bed rest. He was told to complete the course of penicillin prescribed to him at the hospital but no further treatment was required.

A year that had started with so much promise had not lived up to expectations. Freddie failed to wrestle the world title from Gus Lesnevich and took two savage beatings from much heavier men in Bruce Woodcock and Joe Baksi.

Travelling back to London from Bournemouth after his first family Christmas without his father Tom, Freddie made a resolution for 1947. There would be no more heavyweight fights. As soon as he spoke to Ted, he would tell him he only really wanted one fight: a rematch with Lesnevich for the light-heavyweight championship of the world.

Having lost three out of the four fights since leaving the RAF, he would have to work hard to rebuild his reputation. He had to quickly get back to winning ways. As the coming year would prove, this would be easier said than done.

14

Done a runner

THE telephone rang at Broadribb's home. It was Nat Seller. 'He's only gone and done a runner, Ted. I've had enough of him.' It was the third day in a row that the old trainer had turned up at Jack Solomon's gym and there was no sign of Freddie.

For Broadribb, it was the straw that broke the camel's back. Not only had Freddie embarrassed himself by quitting against Baksi, he had then had the front to say that he no longer wanted to face heavyweights. He was happier in the light-heavyweight division, even though it would cost his handlers money.

Speaking on the phone to Seller, Broadribb seethed. Freddie did not realise how much work he had put into convincing Jack Solomons to allow Freddie to campaign as a light-heavyweight. After the performances against Woodcock and Baksi, Jack needed some persuading that Freddie was really at world-class level.

'All he needs is a few fights back at light-heavy to build his confidence,' insisted Broadribb. 'He went down ill with malaria while serving in India and it took him time to recover.' Broadribb used every excuse he could think of just to keep on the right side of Solomons.

In the end, the promoter stopped short of dropping Freddie. 'I suppose he has only ever lost to the world champion at light-heavyweight and it was his first fight back after serving overseas. If he can start winning again then we should be able to get him into a world title fight, but if he loses again then that's the end of him.'

Once a fight had been signed with Dutch light-heavyweight champion Willi Quentemeyer for 20 January 1947, Broadribb gave Freddie a stern talking to. There were to be no more petty rows with Nat Seller. He had to listen to what his trainer told him and follow it to the letter. Duggie Bygrave was also told that if he saw Freddie slacking, he was to tell Broadribb immediately.

After losing to both Woodcock and Baksi in his last two fights, Freddie was ready to listen and get down to some hard work. In the first few days of January, he ran upwards of eight miles a day then sparred somewhere in the region of 15 to 20 rounds with Bygrave before ending the day with a full massage. Each night, he was in bed by 9pm.

Everything went well until ten days before the fight. Seller reported back to Broadribb that Freddie was fighting fit and already bang on the light-heavyweight limit. But the next time Ted heard from Nat, he was told that Freddie had disappeared.

'I thought things were going well?' Broadribb asked the trainer.

'They were – then he didn't show up on Monday or since. His landlady hasn't seen him for days.'

Broadribb thanked Seller and put the phone down. He put his hand against his forehead. The fight was only days away. If he could not find Freddie, he would have to tell Jack the bout was off. Not only would it mean Broadribb was out of pocket, but any fighters he managed in future would be barred from appearing on Solomons' bills.

Sitting in his lounge, Broadribb risked the very real possibility of losing his livelihood because of Mills. He was going to track him down and physically drag him to the ring if he had to. In the end, it was not hard to find him. He was back home in Bournemouth with his mother.

After speaking with Lottie over the phone, Ted immediately drove to Terrace Road, where he found Freddie ill in bed. 'Fight's off, I'm afraid, I feel like shit. I've been in bed since I got here.'

Broadribb hit the roof. He could not believe Freddie's nonchalant attitude. 'There is no fucking way we are postponing this fight. Either you get up and get in the car with me right now or you will never, ever fight in London again.'

'Leave it out, Ted, I've been throwing up for days, there's no way I can fight,' said Freddie.

'Okay, okay, we can postpone the fight as long as you can stump up the grand you owe Quentemeyer for wasting his time.'

Lying there, Freddie knew he had no real choice. He did not have the money to pay Broadribb and boxing was his only means of income. He could not risk being put on some sort of blacklist. So, despite suffering from the effects of influenza, within the hour he was sat wrapped up in the passenger seat of Broadribb's car on the way back to London. From now on, Freddie would stay at Broadribb's house in Shepperton to ensure he was never tempted to run away again.

It was clear to Ted that Freddie was ill but he hoped regular massages of wintergreen and Vick's vapour rub would help ensure his boxer was close to full fitness come fight night.

Things were made worse for Broadribb later that evening when Jack Solomons rang. 'A little bird tells me Freddie has gone walk about. Is this true?'

'No, no, he's fine. He's with me now. He had a little cold but he's over the worst. Just needed a few days break. He will be back in full training tomorrow.'

'That's good. I was planning on popping into the gym to take a look at him. See you tomorrow.'

A big right connected with Duggie Bygrave's jaw and he was on the floor. Broadribb turned to Solomons and smiled. Freddie looked a million dollars throwing that punch. However, appearances can be deceptive. What Solomons did not know was that Bygrave had been told to take a dive from the first decent shot Freddie threw as soon as Solomons walked in.

Satisfied by what he had seen. Solomons told Freddie that Quentemeyer was only a stepping stone and the real prize was a re-match with Lesnevich. He was expecting an early night for Freddie in two days' time.

Standing on the weighing scales at the familiar Royal Albert Hall, Freddie felt worse than ever. Every muscle in his body ached, he was running a high temperature and suffered from a head cold. 'Look at him, he's scared to death,' Broadribb told Freddie pointing at the Dutchman.

For once, all Freddie could think about was getting the fight over and done with as early as possible. He dreamed of a warm bath, hot lemon and climbing into his bed. The last place he wanted to be was a boxing ring.

As Mills waited in his dressing room, he caught a glimpse of himself in the mirror. He was still in his 20s but the influenza made him feel a lot older. His eyes were glazed and his white complexion matched the colour of the towel around his neck.

The Vaseline that had been applied to his face to make his skin more elastic and slippery, and less likely to tear, made him look as though he had been embalmed.

Finally, he made his way to the ring. His sinuses were hurting. He could hardly hear the crowd as his ears were blocked. His eyes were sensitive to the huge arc lights over the ring.

As the bell rung for the first round, Mills hoped Jack Solomons was right and he would be in for an early night. The fight started with both fighters beginning cautiously, Quentemeyer respecting his opponent's power and Mills looking to conserve his limited energy reserves. Mills flicked out his left but the Dutchman bobbed and weaved away. The round ended without any real action from either fighter.

As Mills sat on his stool for the interval, he said nothing. He was focused on finding an opening. On the evidence of the first round, the Dutchman would have presented no real threat to a fully fit Mills. But hindered by influenza, there was a possibility this could be a very long night for the Bournemouth man.

At the start of the second round, Quentemeyer, confident after the guarded opener, came out quickly, catching Mills with a right to the head that hurt and stunned him. Not having the power to hit back immediately, Mills kept to the middle of the ring and waited for his moment.

He did not have to wait long as an over-confident Quentemeyer tried the same trick again only to miss, exposing his jaw in the process. That was all Mills needed and a wicked left hook sent the Dutchman to his knees. He immediately jumped up and walked straight into a copybook right hook, rendering him unconscious before he hit the floor. Ten seconds later, the referee confirmed Mills the winner by knockout in the second round.

'This must be your lucky venue, Freddie,' Broadribb smiled as he put his arms around his man. Freddie had lengthened his winning streak at the Royal Albert Hall.

The first person Broadribb sought out was the promoter Jack Solomons. 'See that, Jack? Laid low for most of the week then he just walks through the guy like that.'

There was no doubt in Solomon's mind just how good Freddie had been. If he could knock out the Dutch champion after being ill, what could he do when he was well? There was another reason why Jack was impressed. It felt as though Freddie was back home fighting in his home town of Bournemouth. The Royal Albert Hall crowd were clearly fanatical about him. Every punch Freddie threw was met with a loud cheer from those assembled.

Therefore, wanting to cash in on Freddie's popularity at the venue, he was back there a month later under the Solomons' promotional banner. His opponent this time was the light-heavyweight champion of Italy, Enrico Bertola.

Showing no ill effects from his recent bout of 'flu, Freddie started in much the same way as he had against Quentemeyer, cautiously assessing the Italian. Bertola got the action started with a flurry of punches that caught Mills mainly on the forearms and shoulders. When Bertola finally did manage to get through, he did not hit Freddie with anything that unduly worried him.

Throughout these rounds, Mills circled around the Italian. He did not really come alive until the third, when he tore into Bertola with both hands, decisively winning the round and giving the visitor plenty to think about.

There were a few gasps in the crowd when Bertola appeared to gain the upper hand in the fourth by pushing Mills back on the ropes. In reality, it was all smoke and mirrors as the Italian flailed away without really having his man in serious trouble. However, some sections of the crowd started to get behind the underdog and, to Freddie's surprise, began to chant Bertola's name.

Sensing he had to put on a bit of a show, Freddie started firing back. Bringing the fight to the centre of the ring, he instinctively knew that Bertola had given his all. He had punched himself out and was hanging on to Freddie in an effort to slow down the pace. At the end of the round, a tiring Bertola lazily walked on to a Mills left hook and was on the canvas just as the bell rang for the end of the round.

During the break, as Mills looked across and saw the Italian's cornermen frantically trying to revive him, Freddie was confident the end was nigh. He was right. Another wicked left hook at the beginning of the round left Bertola helpless on the floor and the referee reached the count of ten. The Italian had made a valiant effort but he was never in Freddie's class.

Just two years later, Enrico Bertola was matched with heavyweight Lee Oma. In a bruising encounter, the mismatched Italian was endlessly pounded by the bigger man. After losing a unanimous decision, he lost consciousness and fell into a coma.

Despite the doctors' best efforts to save him, he died the next day following brain surgery. He was just 27 years old. Years later, Freddie would pay tribute to Bertola as a gallant fighter and brave man.

For someone still struggling for money, the lure of the biggest purse of his career was too strong to resist. Within a few weeks, Freddie was on a plane bound for Johannesburg with Broadribb to face the South African heavyweight Johnny Ralph. The money on offer was enough of a temptation for Freddie to go back on his word never to fight heavyweights again.

At Freddie's suggestion, former South African heavyweight Don McCorkindale accompanied them on the trip.

As well as acting as Freddie's sparring partner and trainer, as Nat Seller had stayed at home, McCorkindale needed to get away from it all. He had been devastated to discover that his wife Chrissie, who was also Broadribb's daughter, had been having an affair. Having told him she was leaving him for the other man, she had filed for divorce. Training Freddie would take his mind off things.

The press in South Africa talked excitedly of Freddie's arrival. The bout with Johnny Ralph would be the first time their man had shared a ring with a world-class opponent. Ralph had captured the imagination of the boxing public in South Africa in a way no one else had ever managed previously.

In only his eighth professional fight, he had become the South African heavyweight champion by knocking out Nick Wolmarans. A win against American Buddy Scott had led some excitable newspapermen in his native South Africa to talk of Ralph fighting Joe Louis. If he could beat Freddie, it would prove he was ready for the best men in the division.

Things did not go according to plan for Freddie once he arrived. The food disagreed with him and several days were lost because of a stomach bug. Just as he recovered, news came through that Ralph had been injured.

While reaching out to catch a ball in a back yard game of cricket with friends, Ralph had fallen, spraining his wrist and breaking his finger. The fight was postponed for a fortnight to allow Ralph time to recover. It could not have come at a worse time. Struggling with the heat and feeling homesick, Freddie did not know how much longer he could stay in South Africa.

To fill the time, Mills and McCorkindale engaged in some exhibition matches. It was at one of these where Freddie finally met Ralph. The cast on the South African's arm indicated to Mills that they would not be fighting any time soon.

Not wanting a wasted journey, Ted Broadribb came up with a new plan. With only two weeks' notice, the man who had been beaten by Ralph for the South African heavyweight title, Nick Wolmarans, stepped into the breach.

Like Mills, Wolmarans was a natural light-heavyweight but he had never really been in with anyone of the calibre of the Englishman.

The fight was to be held at an open-air ground at the Johannesburg greyhound track, called Wembley. By the time Freddie entered the ring, he wanted to get out of the country as quickly as possible. The training facilities were not as good as those back home and the locals had not been very friendly, barracking him at open training sessions. Since the stomach trouble, he had been too afraid to touch the food.

Deciding to channel some of his frustrations into his fight with Wolmarans, Freddie tore into the South African. Opening up with some wicked body shots, Wolmarans looked visibly panicked as he tied Freddie up and tried to stop some of his best work.

By the second round, it was clear that the South African did not have the power to trouble Freddie. This did not mean Mills had it all his own way. By the third, Wolmarans began to trade punches in the centre of the ring. In the clinches, there was no hiding place. Wolmarans was breathing heavily, he didn't have the strength to push Freddie back and he only released his hold when the referee said break.

By the fourth, Mills was punching at will, although Wolmarans stayed on his feet, his face showing the effects of Freddie's two-fisted aggression. By the end of the round, Wolmarans bled heavily from the mouth and nose.

If the South African was not putting up much of the fight, the altitude was certainly affecting Freddie. He sensed that Wolmarans was tiring but he was getting short of breath himself and was taking in big gulps of air between rounds. In the fifth, every two-handed attack Mills launched sapped his energy. The Briton was beginning to question whether he could last much longer. He decided to end the fight as soon as the chance arose.

It would not be too long and a right hook to the jaw brought Wolmarans to his knees. He was quickly up but once Freddie had a man down he very rarely let them off the hook. He cornered the South African, who took 20 unanswered blows before he sank to the floor. Bravely, he got back to his feet before a final left hook ended the bout.

As the referee counted Wolmarans out, Freddie's thoughts turned to London. South Africa had not been a great experience and he could not wait to return home. The pictures in the press the next day told the story. Despite winning the bout, Freddie looked fed up. Two days later, he was back on the plane. 'When am I going to get some decent opposition, Ted? I've earned my spurs. I think I'm ready for Lesnevich.'

As the plane left Johannesburg Airport, Ted sat back in his seat and said, 'Soon, very soon.' Like Freddie, he could not wait to get back but for different reasons. He knew Jack Solomons had lined up a world title eliminator for Freddie and he hoped he would soon be on the road to managing a world champion. But it was going to be much tougher than either he or Freddie could have imagined.

15

Lucky punch

IT was a brilliant idea. The colour bar on black fighters contesting British titles had just been lifted and Jack Solomons had thought of a way of turning it to his advantage. How about putting on a black versus white bill at Harringay Arena, with Freddie headlining against a leading contender from the United States of America?

He would promote the fight as the final eliminator for a world title shot against Gus Lesnevich. Firstly, he had to find the right type of fighter. After the performances against Woodcock and Baksi, it had been difficult getting Freddie back into the picture. He had looked good in his previous three outings but there were still doubts about his punch resistance against higher-class opposition.

The opponent had to be good but not too dangerous. Picking up the phone to his American counterpart in New York, Mike Jacobs, Solomons went over the options. Archie Moore was ruled out straight away. The knockout artist represented too much of a risk. Ezzard Charles was deemed far too slick and in any case was more interested in pursuing the heavyweight championship than facing Freddie.

'Okay, what about Lloyd Marshall? His best days are behind him but he would be a good name on your man's record,' Jacobs told Solomons.

Having been a victim of the colour bar, Lloyd Marshall was one of the best fighters never to win a world title. He was acknowledged as a member of *Murderers' Row*, an unofficial stable of black contenders renowned for their innate toughness and superior boxing skill. Their number included some of the most avoided fighters in the world.

By the time Jacobs agreed to bring Marshall to the UK, he was seen as over the hill. His best performances were during the war. He had been knocked out in two of his last three fights and had laboured to a 15-round decision in his last bout. It seemed to some observers as though the punching power he had demonstrated on his way to beating the likes of Joey Maxim and Jake LaMotta early in his career had deserted him.

'Make it look good, Fred. Carry him for a few rounds. This will only be a warm-up for Lesnevich,' Ted told Freddie just before they met the Ohio fighter to sign the contracts.

Up close, Freddie thought Marshall showed his age. The American had only just stepped off the plane and Freddie was sure he saw some grey hairs on Marshall's unshaven face. Perhaps it was the jet lag from the flight, but Marshall did not seem too friendly, 'What do you think of London, pal?' Freddie smiled.

Flashing Mills a menacing glare, Marshall replied, 'Ain't your city, dingy?'

'Yes, wars are a bit of a bother sometimes,' replied Freddie meekly.

Once the ink was dry on the contract, the two shook hands. 'I haven't come all this way to be your patsy. You better be ready come fight night, buddy,' Marshall threatened his opponent through gritted teeth.

If Freddie was concerned, he did not show it when later that night he appeared on the top-rated BBC radio programme *Ignorance is Bliss*, where he was introduced as the housewives' favourite.

A spoof quiz show, Freddie happily played along with the rest of the cast as a slow, dim-witted boxer. Near the end of the show, Freddie told listeners to tune in in a fortnight's time to cheer him on, promising to 'spank the Yank'.

Both fighters set up camp at Jack Solomons' gymnasium, although they never met there. Marshall was given the morning session while Freddie did his roadwork. The afternoon was handed over to the Mills team, which consisted of Nat Seller and the ever-faithful Duggie Bygrave.

'Why do you keep crossing your feet, Freddie?' Nat shouted from the ring apron as Duggie caught Freddie off balance in sparring. In the first few days, it seemed as though Freddie's gift for great footwork had deserted him.

Both Bygrave and Seller had noticed it when Freddie was skipping. There were times when he found it impossible to get a good rhythm going. On other occasions, the heavy leather rope became tangled around his legs.

In sparring, he found it difficult to get any of his shots off. There was no power behind his hooks and he found it almost impossible to plant his feet on the ground. 'I just don't know, Nat. I think the heat in South Africa affected me more than I thought,' said Freddie.

'I think you're doing too much, you just need to take it easy.' Nat suggested to Freddie that he brought his sparring with Duggie to a close and concentrated on his physical fitness.

For the next ten days, Freddie began every day with a run and a few stretches then hit the heavy bag every afternoon. Both Ted and Jack were reporting back that Marshall was looking slow and sluggish in training and had even been knocked down by his sparring partners a few times. There was absolutely nothing to worry about, Ted reassured Freddie.

That's not what Tommy Reddington told Freddie when he came to the gym to visit his old friend the day before the fight. 'I watched Marshall train this morning. You are going to have to be careful, Freddie. He has a whole variety of punches, a beautiful little body roll and looks in tip-top condition.'

There was little Freddie could do this close to the fight. After speaking with Reddington, his confidence hit an all-time low. Seeking reassurance from Broadribb, Freddie was told, yes, Marshall looked good but they had to bring in replacement sparring partners because the original ones were knocking seven bells out of him.

Broadribb said Marshall had been having such a bad time of it that his management wanted to pull him out and catch the first flight home. It was only thanks to Solomons' powers of persuasion that he stayed. Even though Freddie listened, it did nothing to lift his spirits. There was something wrong and he could not quite put his finger on it.

Silence lingered as Freddie travelled to Harringay Arena in Ted's car. This was nothing unusual. Freddie was usually quiet before big fights. He liked the silence to focus his mind and prepare for the battle ahead. This time, he was seriously worried. Who was telling the truth, Tommy or Ted? He knew he was not ready and Marshall was an unknown quantity. Silently, he said a little prayer hoping Marshall was indeed over the hill.

The dressing room was deathly quiet. Normally Freddie would have a rub-down from Nat before putting on his gear. There would be a few rounds of shadow boxing to warm up then he would be ready for the buzzer, which signalled it was his turn to enter the ring. Tonight, he did not want to do any of that. Upon his arrival at the arena, Freddie was moody and sullen. Walking straight past his dressing room, he went to sit in the audience to watch the undercard.

As the clocked ticked towards the appointed hour, Nat Seller became frantic. 'He's gone and done another runner. I knew it,' the trainer screamed at Ted Broadribb.

Going into the crowd, Ted found Freddie. Putting a hand on his shoulder, he said, 'Come on, son, you are going to be late.' Mills did not reply, silently standing up to follow his manager to the dressing room. There was no time for a massage or any shadow boxing as Freddie quickly changed into his boots and shorts. Nat Seller said nothing as he laced up Freddie's gloves. He had seen that look on his fighter's face before and knew better than to break the silence with a wisecrack.

Once the buzzer went, Broadribb helped Freddie put on his dressing gown. A white towel covered his mop of black curly hair. The Harringay Arena was in complete darkness. Apart from the spotlight on Freddie, the only light was provided by cigarettes from spectators.

In the ring, Broadribb whispered in Freddie's ear, 'You better fucking win this. Jack's having a bad night. He's already lost four matches tonight. Don't make it a fifth.' Freddie shook his head. Is that all Ted cared about? Not upsetting Jack?

Fuck those two old men. He was going to hurt Marshall tonight, Freddie thought as the bell sounded to begin the fight. As the combatants came out, Freddie began circling his opponent, taking his time. Marshall opened proceedings while Mills tried to keep his distance.

Out of nowhere, a crushing left hook to the right eye from the American temporarily paralysed Mills. Such was the power of the punch that Freddie felt he had been shot. The pain was instant and unbearable. Unable to respond, Freddie was helpless, at the mercy of the American.

Not realising the damage he had inflicted on his opponent, Marshall backed off. Calmly, he danced around Freddie throwing accurate jabs to the face of the hurt fighter. The whole side of Freddie's face seared with pain. Blinking in an attempt to clear his vision, for the first time in his career Freddie thought about taking a knee in the hope of unscrambling his senses.

His pride and his courage would never let him do that. Trying to stay out of range, Freddie offered no resistance. He feared if he went in too close he would be open to more punishment from Marshall, who had ferocious power. Tommy Reddington had been right. Marshall was in marvellous fighting shape.

Sitting on the stool between rounds, Freddie pleaded with Ted, 'I'm going blind. I'm going blind. You have to stop this, Ted.' Freddie was now in a panic. He remembered Percy Cook telling him on his milk round how his brother Gordon had lost an eye in the ring. He saw many booth fighters lose their sight. He lived in fear of going the same way.

'It's nothing, stop crying like a baby. He got lucky. Go out there and show him what you can do,' replied Broadribb, sending his fighter out for the second round.

All Freddie could do was return to the brawling, roughhouse boxer he instinctively was. Biting down hard on his gum shield, Freddie waded into Marshall's body. A big right to the stomach momentarily winded the American but it was the Ohio fighter who dominated the round. Targeting the right eye with accurate jabs and an awesome left hand, Marshall went about clinically dismantling Mills.

The American danced around Mills with good lefts. Freddie tried to tie him up, throwing short rights. On numerous occasions, Mills was told to break by the referee, which eventually led to Freddie receiving a warning. Right at the end of the round a pulverising left hook caught Freddie flush on the jaw, sending him down. He jumped up at the count of one. Mercifully, the bell rang to bring the second round to a close before Marshall could inflict any more damage.

'Please, Ted, I can't go on. Every punch hurts. I've nothing left. Pull me out.' Freddie was now begging his manager to stop the contest.

Broadribb wouldn't hear of it. The chances of fighting for the world championship were hanging by a thread. Imploring Freddie to get to work on Marshall's body, he pushed him out for the next round.

Unsurprisingly, the third round was nothing but a disaster. In a vain attempt to hold on to the advancing Marshall, Mills took a shot just under his heart that put him on the floor. Freddie did not see it as he was practically blind in his right eye. The punch sucked all the air out of his lungs and it took a huge effort to climb off the canvas after a count of nine.

The eye injury, together with the balance problems he had been suffering in training, took his main weapons away from him. Throwing huge windmill-like punches was not the answer. Marshall was too slippery and slick to be caught by a random haymaker.

By the middle of the round, Marshall was landing punches at will and three unanswered right hands put Mills on his knees again for a count of five. Known as a body puncher himself, Mills was taking a dose of his own medicine as Marshall's spiteful digs downstairs were beginning to tell.

By the end of the round, Mills had visited the canvas again after another huge left hook from Marshall. The American's power and speed were just too much.

Still Mills, digging deep into the reserves of courage he was famous for, came out for the fourth showing flashes of his old self. He managed to throw some good-looking left hooks but there was little power behind them as Marshall's wicked body punches had sapped him of his strength.

Halfway through the round, a hurt and tired Freddie reverted to holding. The referee warned him yet again for excessive clinching.

The paying public wanted a fight and it did not matter how hurt one of the fighters was. After being broken up by the referee, Mills, who had lost his ability to get out of the way of punches, suffered some heavy punishment. Only a hard right managed to hold a swarming Marshall back as he sought to end the fight.

'What was that?' Broadribb asked Freddie upon on his return to the corner at the end of the round. 'Don't you want to be world champ?'

'Just stop the fight, I've had it,' replied an exhausted Freddie.

'The only way this fight is getting stopped is if Marshall knocks you out,' Broadribb said. He had lost patience with Freddie and was convinced he was not trying. The manager wondered how the hell he would face Solomons after this performance.

The end was as swift as it was brutal. Freddie was largely unable to see, suffering from dizziness and double vision, and in severe pain from every blow landed by the American. A smashing left hook, similar to the one which did all the damage in the first round, sent Mills to the floor for the fourth and final time. This time there was no getting back up and Freddie, despite a valiant attempt, failed to beat the count. The referee waved the contest off and Mills gladly accepted defeat.

Watching from his corner, Broadribb was angry, 'See that, Nat, he just quit and gave up.'

'There is something wrong with that boy,' replied Nat. 'I've been telling you that for months.'

Finally back on his feet, Freddie walked over to his corner. If he was expecting any sympathy, he received none. 'You're a fucking disgrace. I've wasted my time on you,' Broadribb hissed at Freddie. Nat Seller simply shook his head.

The victor came over and commiserated with Freddie. He was sure the outcome would have been much different had he not caught Freddie with what he termed a lucky punch in the first round.

'The punch may have been lucky for you but not for me,' Freddie quipped before returning on his own to an empty dressing room.

After beating Freddie, Marshall faded into obscurity. He was knocked out in a third meeting with Ezzard Charles and went on to lose half of his remaining fights. He never got the chance to fight Lesnevich for the world light-heavyweight championship.

The dressing room was not empty for long. Within minutes of lying down on the rub-down table, in burst Jack Solomons with Broadribb and Seller in tow. 'How you feeling, champ?' the promoter asked Freddie sarcastically.

'Do you know how much your little performance in the ring just cost me? Nine fucking grand. You know when I wanted to drop you after Baksi, it was Ted who talked me around and this is how you repay us, by quitting in the ring?'

'How the fuck am I am going to get Lesnevich to come over now? What am I going to say to him? Come over to England and beat up the human punch bag Fearless Freddie fucking Mills? Who the fuck will want to buy tickets to see that? You should be fucking ashamed of yourself.'

After ten minutes of ranting and raving, Solomons finally left Freddie alone with Broadribb and Seller. 'I think we should both leave you alone to think about your future, Freddie. You can make your own way back home tonight.' After closing the door, Freddie heard the two men's footsteps as they walked away from the dressing room, leaving him with his thoughts.

For an hour, still dressed in his boxing gear, he lay on the table just thinking about the past 18 months and all the losses he had suffered. Up until tonight, all of them could be easily explained away.

Against Gus Lesnevich, Mills had taken the fight after a long lay-off. It was his first match after the war and, of course, the American was a world champion. In the middle rounds, Mills was very much on top and had the referee not stopped the fight with only four seconds left in the tenth round, Freddie might have regrouped and beaten the American.

As for Bruce Woodcock, it had just come too soon after the Lesnevich fight. It was still a half-decent performance. Freddie had damaged Woodcock's eye and was never down in the fight. Joe Baksi was just too big. Mills had given too much weight away, he was always the underdog and no one had expected him to win anyway.

But the loss against Marshall was different. Freddie was the bigger man. Even though Marshall had been in with better opposition, he had been knocked out in two out of his last three fights. He was handpicked by Solomons, who believed he was on the slide. Freddie was expected to win yet it was the American who dominated.

In the darkness of the dressing room, Freddie mulled over the same question again and again. Was he washed up?

His mind went back to the night he seconded for Gypsy Daniels against a fighter called Cyril Ellis nearly ten years before. The man who had beaten Max Schmeling took a real hammering for three rounds. At the end of it, Freddie was practically crying, begging Daniels to stop. He would not listen. Was this to be Freddie's fate, another boxer who did not know when he had had enough?

This fight, more than any other, hurt Freddie. For the first time since he started out, he had no answer to his opponent's vicious punching power. There were no excuses. It seemed as though his legendary punch resistance had deserted him and without it he would be a vulnerable fighter.

A miserable journey back home saw Freddie stick his thumb out on the deserted roads for hours before a friendly truck driver picked him up. Once back at his digs, Mills spent a restless night vomiting while applying an ice pack to his injured eye.

First thing the following morning, Freddie was again in front of his GP. 'I think you have broken your orbital bone, Mr Mills,' the doctor informed him before referring him to the local hospital for an X-ray.

'If I have broken the orbital bone, what does it mean?'

'Probably an operation. You should be fully recovered in a year to 18 months.'

'What about my boxing career?'

'My dear boy, you should never fight again.'

Freddie was in shock. After thanking the doctor, he left with a piece of paper in his hand, an appointment with the radiology department. Self-pity turned to anger. No doctor was going to tell him to retire, so he scrunched up the bit of paper and threw it in the bin. Somehow, some way, he was going to find a way back to the top.

On the way home, Freddie picked up the morning newspaper. Tucked away under the headlines informing the country of his poor performance against Marshall was an interview with Nat Seller.

Talking to a journalist in the aftermath of the fight, Seller said Freddie had been struggling to re-acclimatise from the altitude of South Africa. Typically, rather than rest, he had been eager to get in the ring as soon as possible, so he pushed Broadribb into making the fight with Marshall.

Despite repeated warnings that he was training too much, Freddie threw himself into sparring and roadwork. By the time he climbed into the ring, the effects of a gruelling training camp and the altitude had combined to leave him exhausted. That is why Freddie had put on such a poor show.

The paper also carried a quote from Jack Solomons, who said he was still hopeful of a return match with Gus Lesnevich but first Freddie would have to rebuild his career by going after the European light-heavyweight crown, then chase world honours. It was the sort of news that lifted Freddie's sprits. His career wasn't over. There was still much to be achieved.

16

Last chance

AS the referee fastened the European light-heavyweight championship around Freddie's waist, Broadribb was ecstatic. His arms were in the air and with a huge grin on his face he declared, 'That was fantastic, Freddie. Next stop, Gus Lesnevich.'

It had all been so different two months before. In the aftermath of the Lloyd Marshall bout, Freddie had been desperate to get hold of Ted. For days, Broadribb had refused to take any phone calls from Freddie and telegrams went unanswered.

When Freddie paid a visit to Jack Solomons' gymnasium in the hope of bumping into his manager, he was told by two heavies that he was not welcome there.

Perhaps it was his state of mind but he was sure he had heard two boys who were sparring in the ring call him a coward and quitter as he forlornly left the gymnasium, where only days before he had been preparing for a world title eliminator.

The longer Freddie did not hear from Ted, the more depression tightened its grip over him. All sorts of dark thoughts swirled around Freddie's mind. He was a fighter and if he could not fight then he was nothing, worthless.

Sitting in his digs, he realised he had not been through the door for days. The curtains were pulled as a migraine made him sensitive to light. He could not remember the last time he enjoyed a good night's sleep. Wanting to ease the pain, he went to the medicine cabinet and opened a bottle of sleeping pills.

His hands shaking from the headache, he dropped the glass container, scattering the tablets all over the floor. Getting down on his hands and knees, Freddie began to scoop them up in his hands. It was then that he thought about swallowing them all. That way, the pain would go away forever.

Freddie lined up the pills along the kitchen counter and poured himself a glass of water. He sat there contemplating what he was going to do when there was a knock on the door.

It was his landlady. 'Freddie, Freddie, you have a phone call. It's a bloke. He says it's important.'

Whatever Freddie was planning to do was soon forgotten about. Within seconds, he was in the hallway answering the phone. It was Ted Broadribb.

'Hello Ted, where you been hiding?' Freddie cheerily asked his manager.

It was clear Broadribb was in no mood for small talk. 'We need to talk. My place tomorrow at midday. Okay?'

'Okay,' replied Freddie. He could tell by the tone of Broadribb's voice that this was serious.

Lying in bed that night, Freddie rehearsed what he was going to say over and over again. The Marshall fight was just an off night. He made one mistake and was caught with a lucky punch. He had come back from South Africa ill and, not wanting to let anyone down, had taken the fight when he shouldn't have.

He hoped Broadribb would accapt his excuses and give him another chance. The only alternative to professional boxing was to go back on the booths. As hard as his last few fights had been, being on the fairgrounds was tough and he did not want to return there, least of all as a 'has-been', someone the local hard man could brag about to his friends, 'Hey fellas, I beat up Freddie Mills.'

It was an apprehensive Freddie who knocked on Ted's door in Shepperton ten minutes before the appointed time. Broadribb did not say anything as he answered the door, simply motioning him to come in.

With a blackened, swollen eye and lips that were twice their normal size, Freddie was still bearing the bruises from Marshall's fists. Finally, Broadribb spoke, 'Freddie, you fucked up, you made a fool out of me and have cost Jack money. I think it's best for all concerned you pack it in.'

The frustrations of the past few days boiled over and Freddie broke down in tears. 'No, please Ted, I don't know anything else. Boxing's all I got.'

'Give me one good reason why I should carry on managing you? You're a quitter,' Broadribb snapped.

As Freddie begged his manager for one more chance, he was unaware of the conversation Broadribb had had with Jack Solomons before he picked up the phone to him.

Sitting in Solomons' offices at Great Windmill Street, Broadribb had discussed Freddie's future. 'He's fucked me over, Ted. He cost me money.'

'Look, he's still box office. Why don't you give him a run-out against Pol Gouffax, the European champion? If he loses, so what? You make money on the gate. If he wins, you can sell him as the European champion against Lesnevich.'

After offering Freddie a handkerchief to dry his tears and a cup of tea, Broadribb told Freddie this was absolutely his last chance. It would take hard work but he thought there was an outside chance of Freddie securing a rematch with Gus Lesnevich. But Freddie had to promise to knuckle down.

Broadribb went on to explain to Freddie that the first piece of the jigsaw in building a fight with Lesnevich would be the European light-heavyweight championship against Paul 'Pol' Gouffax.

The handlers of the 1936 Belgian Olympian were keen to match their man with the Englishman. All they were waiting for was Freddie's signature on a contract.

It was too good to be true. Freddie had come to Broadribb's house expecting to be begging for his career. Instead, he was walking away with the opportunity to become European champion. A few days later, Mills was in the Cambridgeshire countryside, hitting the road in the morning while working on the heavy bag in the afternoon. It was an enjoyable camp, made better by the sunshine. Keen to ensure Freddie would not peak too early, Nat Seller instructed his man to stay away from sparring and concentrate on sharpening his skills.

It was therefore a relaxed Freddie who stood on the scales and clapped his eyes on Gouffax for the first time. Despite never having fought outside Holland or Italy, the Belgian could make a claim to being the best light-heavyweight on the European continent. But to Freddie and his trainer, he was very much an unknown quantity.

In his dressing room, the nerves finally hit Freddie. Unbeknown to Seller or Broadribb, Mills had a nagging pain in his neck that felt much worse than just a pulled muscle. No amount of encouragement from trainer or manager could stop

Freddie's mind wandering back to his last fight with Marshall. Superstitious to the last, Freddie even worried about Harringay Arena, a place that had never brought him much luck.

Very soon, all the questions that had played on his mind since being knocked out would be answered. As the buzzer went in his dressing room, signalling he was next on the bill, Freddie was met outside by an upbeat Jack Solomons.

Any fears that Freddie's recent performances might have deterred the public from paying to watch their great hero had proved unfounded as a sell-out crowd waited in anticipation for Britain's biggest boxing star to make his appearance.

Nothing pleased the promoter more than a sell-out crowd. 'This boy is nothing, take him easy. Carry him a few rounds and make it look good. Let's put on a show,' Solomons bellowed at Freddie as he started his walk to the ring.

Freddie wished he shared his promoter's optimism. As he flicked out punches in the air while his name was announced, Freddie could feel the constant pain in his neck drifting down between his shoulder blades.

As soon as the bell rang, any concerns the Belgian was going to cause serious problems evaporated. As Mills advanced, Gouffax began to retreat and as the round progressed it was clear the Belgian respected Freddie's power too much to offer any real offense.

This was the pattern of the fight for the next two rounds, Gouffax running away while Freddie chased him around the ring. Mills swung wildly, hitting thin air as his opponent desperately tried to keep out of range, worsening the pain between his shoulder blades.

Fearful of being forced to retire through injury, Freddie gave up chasing the Belgian in the third round and instead patiently waited for Gouffax to come to him. There was no way the man from the lowlands could continue all night like this. Sooner or later, he had to engage.

After four rounds they finally came together in the middle of the ring, where Freddie was at his most comfortable and did the greatest damage. The first decent shot of the night came from Mills, a heavy right hook to the side of the head that saw the Belgian crumble to the canvas for a count of five.

Sensing blood, Freddie moved in for the kill. Gouffax did not have the skill to get out of the way of the flurry of punches Mills threw to head and body, nor the chin to withstand the punishment. But he showed great heart, getting up after being knocked down a further five times.

As Freddie rushed in looking for the one punch that would finally break his duck at Harringay, the Belgian decided he had had enough of waving his gloves in the air. Sportingly, he walked over to Freddie and lifted his hand, declaring him the winner of the fight.

For the paying public it was a frustrating bout, but for Freddie it was the perfect antidote after Lloyd Marshall. Not only had he shown he still had knockout power but he was now the best light-heavyweight on the European continent. All in all, it was a good night's work.

'You are the star, Freddie, you're the one they all want. That performance will make Lesnevich sit up and take notice. Told you you still had it,' a triumphant Broadribb told Freddie as he left the ring.

Once back in the dressing room, Jack Solomons confirmed he was going to cable the United States in the morning telling the Lesnevich camp that Freddie would fight their man anywhere, any time. Freddie was ecstatic. His career was back on track. Perhaps he was right all along. The fight against Lloyd Marshall was just a bad day at the office.

In the post-fight euphoria, Freddie was sure he could wrestle the world title from Lesnevich. Had he not dominated the middle rounds of their first fight? He was sure had the referee not stepped in to end it he would have found a second wind and stopped the American, who was struggling to see such was the beating Freddie had handed out.

After knocking out four of his five opponents since beating Freddie, Lesnevich was being mentioned in the same breath as Jack Sharkey, Joe Louis and Henry Armstrong. His reputation as the best light-heavyweight in the world was underlined when he was voted *The Ring* magazine's Fighter of the Year in 1947.

However, for Lesnevich doubts would remain. Freddie Mills was the only man who had given him trouble at light heavy-weight since the end of the war. Lesnevich had not forgotten how vulnerable he felt that night, in a foreign land, half blind and finding it difficult to breathe with a broken nose.

Could Freddie spring a surprise and beat the former lifeguard? It was an intriguing question that Jack Solomons felt was going to be answered soon enough.

In the end, it came to nothing. Solomons could not pin Lesnevich's management down for a date and Freddie went into months of inactivity, boxing a few exhibition bouts and touring youth clubs. Each week began the same way. A meeting with Broadribb, with assurances from Solomons the American was about to sign a contract, only to be met with disappointment when nothing happened.

Even though it was months since Freddie had appeared in the ring, he retained his popularity. When he visited

Weymouth Amateur Boxing Club, over a thousand boys turned up just to catch a glimpse of their idol.

After talking with the boys and refereeing a few matches, Mills could not leave the venue until he handed out autographs to everyone. Even on this night, Freddie could not escape the question to which frustratingly he had no answer. When are you going to fight for the world title, Mr Mills? In the car on the way back to London, Freddie put the question to his manager.

'When are you gonna get me the fucking fight, Ted? It's costing me money sat on my arse all day.'

'Soon, soon, but Jack wants you to stay active. He has lined up a fight with Stephane Olek.'

'He's a fucking *heavyweight*!'

'Yeah, but he made Bruce Woodcock work over 15 rounds. Take him out and Lesnevich will be ours.'

'You told me after Baksi no more heavyweights. What are you playing at, Ted?'

'Listen, Jack says the Lesnevich people want to see if you can still take a punch. Olek is perfect for us.'

Desperate to lure Gus Lesnevich to the United Kingdom, Freddie signed the contract at Jack Solomons gymnasium. He would once again venture into the land of the giants.

There was torrential rain in Manchester the night of 28 November 1947 and a storm brewed in the ring as Mills charged out from the opening bell. He launched himself at Olek, a great shot connecting flush on the jaw of the Frenchman, who outweighed Freddie by a stone and a half.

This was more like the Freddie who had destroyed Len Harvey in a round. The crowd roared as he waded into Olek, looking to finish it early. When the bell rang to end the round, it seemed only a matter of time before the Frenchman would be on his back.

In the second, Mills looked to finish what he had started in the first. Aggressively working the body, he threw everything with little or no thought for the sweet science of the sport. Olek realised he had to increase the distance between him and Mills, so he patiently worked the jab hard into his opponent's face while at the same time moving out of range.

By the third, Mills' belligerence saw him build up a lead on the judges' cards, although slowly but surely Olek was making his way back into the fight. Each wild attack from Mills ended with the bigger man tying him up, making him unable to work on the inside.

The Frenchman used his weight advantage. Every time the two fighters clinched, he would bear down on Mills' back and neck. It was a testament to Freddie's unflinching courage that he was able to prop up the much heavier Frenchman while suffering from constant pain in his neck and shoulders.

The only thing Freddie was hitting in the middle rounds was thin air as Olek used superior movement and his jab to make the Bournemouth man look clumsy and flat footed.

Rounds seven through to nine saw Freddie being out-thought and outboxed while taking some heavy punches in the process. As the bell sounded for the tenth, he could not be sure whether he had done enough to win the fight. Perhaps Olek felt the same because in the final three minutes they went toe to toe, rocking each other with some of the biggest punches they had thrown. The crowd had certainly got their money's worth as the referee raised Freddie's hand.

According to Broadribb, there was little doubt that Freddie's career was on the up again. He had taken some hard shots but his punch resistance was still there. He had fought fire with fire and nearly stopped the Frenchman in the early rounds. Surely now, Lesnevich would agree to a rematch.

Despite constantly pestering both Broadribb and Solomons for a date with Lesnevich, as 1947 turned into 1948 there was nothing. The Lesnevich camp had not replied to any of the telegrams sent by Jack Solomons. A world title fight seemed nothing more than a pipe dream.

Still, Freddie was the European light-heavyweight champion, a title which had to be defended. Spain's Paco Bueno provided the opposition in his first defence back at Harringay Arena on 17 February 1948.

The Spaniard was certainly game enough and enjoyed a good reputation, holding a decision over former Mills opponent Ken Shaw, but there was nothing else in his record to suggest he would give Mills anything more than a good workout.

Unlike the Olek fight, in which Mills paid the price for starting too quickly, he was far more cautious, throwing out a few jabs to get the measure of his opponent. It quickly became apparent that he was in a different class to the Spaniard.

Towards the end of the first round, Mills showed how spiteful he could be as he began punishing the outclassed Bueno. Such was his control of the fight, it was only a matter of time before he ended the challenge of the valiant Bueno.

The opening Mills had been waiting for was not long in coming. A two-fisted attack went unanswered for over a minute and only ended when a heavy right hook put Bueno down. Bueno was unconscious before he hit the floor and remained there motionless for a full 60 seconds before climbing up to congratulate the victor.

The months rolled on and there was still no word from across the Atlantic, so it was back to Harringay Arena and a familiar opponent, Ken Shaw, in a final eliminator for Bruce Woodcock's British heavyweight title.

Shaw was the man whose lip had been split by Mills in his last fight before being posted to India in 1945. Shaw now resembled matinee idol Clark Gable, having grown a moustache.

'What's this about, Ken?' Freddie said, stroking his top lip as they weighed in at Jack Solomons' gymnasium. 'Don't tell me you like it that way.'

'You should ask,' Ken began to explain. 'Remember the last time we met in early 1945? Well, that split lip you gave me didn't look so hot when it finally healed, so I thought I better keep it that way.'

'Ah well, better luck next time,' Freddie told his opponent as they parted after the weigh-in.

As the heavyweight champion of Scotland, Shaw was extremely popular in his home country. It was a real Battle of Britain affair, with Mills representing England and a large Scottish contingent urging the Dundee man to victory. It was hoped that a good showing from Freddie against Shaw would finally persuade Lesnevich to make the trip from America.

After the bell rang for the first round, it was Shaw rather than the usually more aggressive Freddie who tore into his opponent like a man possessed. The Scot quickly pinned Mills down in the corner with a beautiful right. For his part, Freddie responded with a heavy left hook that put Shaw down for a count of two. It was the perfect start.

As soon as Shaw was upright again, another big right from Mills sent him back down for a count of eight. Freddie was firmly in control, the end was nigh but his final advance was stopped dead in its tracks as soon as he noticed that Shaw had split his lip, the old wound reopening under the barrage of blows.

Unwilling to inflict any more damage on someone he counted as a friend, Freddie exclaimed, 'Ken, Ken, your lip is split badly again.'

Freddie motioned to the referee to stop the fight but the official responded by telling Freddie, 'Box on. I'm the boss here and I will tell you when to stop.'

Knowing Shaw's corner would take one look at the injury and pull their man out as soon as the round was over, Freddie eased up and worked the body until the bell. During the interval, Shaw did indeed retire on account of the cut to his lip.

At the end of the fight, a frustrated Freddie felt he had done everything Broadribb and Solomons had asked of him. As his manager embraced him at the end of the fight, promising him yet again a fight with Lesnevich, Freddie whispered, 'Don't give me no more shit. Get the fucking deal done.'

He would not have to wait long. The Lesnevich camp had seen enough. Upon returning to his dressing room, Jack Solomons held a telegram in his hand. It was from New York City informing Freddie that Gus Lesnevich was intending to arrive in London in July, when he would put his world light-heavyweight championship on the line.

Little did he know it then, but Freddie Mills was about to embark on the most remarkable two years of his professional and personal life.

17

Champion

NAT Seller had seen enough. 'That's the third time you have been caught with a right hook. If young Johnny Williams can catch you that easy, what will Lesnevich do?'

Freddie slumped on his stool at the end of another gruelling sparring session with Welsh heavyweight Johnny Williams. 'I've had enough, let's call it a day.'

'Had enough? You said that yesterday and the day before. What's wrong with you? This is the biggest fight of your life and you are throwing it away.'

'Piss off, Nat!' Freddie hissed before throwing his headguard and gloves down on the floor in disgust, then heading back to his digs at Betchworth in Surrey. 'I don't know what's wrong with him. Something has been troubling him since we got here,' Nat confided to Johnny Williams.

'Just nerves, you know what Freddie is like. He will come good in the end,' Williams reassured the trainer.

There was something much more than nerves troubling Freddie. The headaches that had become a way of life were constant, made worse by every punch his sparring partners, Williams and Lloyd Barnett, caught him with.

The pain in his neck made him feel nauseous, causing him to lie down in a darkened room. It was an effort to get out of bed in the morning for roadwork. Seller was so concerned by Freddie's attitude that he asked Ted Broadribb to make the trip down from London to have a word with him.

After another frustrating day, Ted went around to Freddie's digs. Rather than finding a fighter motivated to embark on the challenge of a lifetime, the old manager encountered a broken man.

'Something isn't right, Ted. I feel every single punch and my head feels like it's going to explode. I have pins and needles running down both arms. Some days, I can hardly lift them above my head. I see shots and I can't defend myself.'

'Look Freddie, it don't get much bigger than this. Lesnevich will set you up for life. The contract is the best offered to a British fighter. We have a lot riding on this.'

With 50,000 estimated to attend the fight in White City and Freddie set to receive 17.5 per cent on the gate and 25 per cent of the television, radio and film rights, it was certainly his biggest payday. However, the fighter himself was inconsolable. 'You've seen what Lesnevich has done in his last couple of fights.

'He'll fucking kill me in this state. I want out.'

'Come on, let's get you to a doctor, see what he says. I'll talk to Nat. We can make changes.'

Sat behind the desk of his Harley Street office, the doctor was scathing. 'Mr Mills, I can now tell you the cause of your headaches and dizziness.

'You have a dislocated vertebrae in your neck. You need to have an operation immediately.'

'What would that entail, doc?' Freddie asked.

'It's a very delicate operation and would include complete bed rest for a period of three to six months,' the doctor explained.

'Are you kidding? He has a big fight in a matter of weeks. There is absolutely no way he can have an operation,' Broadribb interrupted.

'I do not think you appreciate the seriousness of the situation. Should Mr Mills sustain just one heavy blow, it could leave him paralysed or worse.'

'Worse?' Freddie asked.

The doctor then went on to explain that by climbing through the ropes, Freddie faced the very real risk of being killed in the ring. His expert opinion was that he announce his retirement immediately.

On the way back to Ted's house, Broadribb tried to talk Freddie round. What did the doctors know? They had always been anti-boxing anyway. He should pay no attention.

Besides, he knew a fantastic bone manipulator, Eddie Mallet, who could run the rule over Freddie. He would be at Ted's house within the hour. After a period of time being pushed and pulled in all directions, Mallet announced he had corrected the displaced vertebrae and Freddie was fit to fight.

When Freddie returned to camp, neither Seller nor his sparring partners were aware of his condition. Mallet had joined the camp, putting Freddie on course of intense manipulation and massage that temporarily left him feeling much better.

After a much-improved session back, Nat told Freddie there would be no more slinking off to bed early. Each day after sparring, they would sit together to watch Freddie's old fights on a projector Broadribb had bought at the insistence of the trainer.

Night after night, they would watch Freddie's bout with Bruce Woodcock and the first fight with Lesnevich, as well all of the American's title defences.

'You gotta watch that right of his, Freddie. He'll take your head off with it,' commented Seller as they watched Lesnevich dispatch his last two opponents in a round.

Remembering the right hand that exploded on his jaw in the tenth round two years earlier, Freddie replied, 'He's a fucking monster, Nat. I gotta keep out of range, get him to throw his right and get in with a couple of punches of my own.'

As Freddie finalised his game plan, the word from the Lesnevich camp only boosted his confidence. At 33, the American was struggling at light-heavyweight and had taken to using Turkish baths and saunas to sweat off the excess weight.

Of the two fighters who met at the weigh-in, it was Freddie who looked most comfortable. His skin glowed, his stomach taut and tight. Lesnevich, on the other hand, looked gaunt and drained. There had been reports in the press for weeks that Lesnevich was really struggling to make the weight. The weighing scale reflected this, with Freddie coming in at a lean 12st 2lbs 8oz and Lesnevich a quarter of a pound under the 12st 7lb limit.

After the weights of both fighters were announced, Jack Solomons made an announcement to the assembled press gallery, 'Ladies and gentlemen of the press, interest in the fight has been so great and the expected crowds so vast, I have asked London's finest, the Metropolitan Police, to escort both fighters to White City tonight.'

Back at Broadribb's house after the weigh-in, Freddie paced around. The pains were back and no amount of manipulation or heat from a sun lamp would make them go away.

As the minutes ticked away, Mills felt sick to the pit of his stomach. There was a numbness and tingling in his arm and the pain in his neck was even more intense than before.

Any thoughts of pulling out soon disappeared as Freddie left Broadribb's home to be greeted by hundreds of adoring fans, who had lined the street to glimpse their hero as he made his way to the biggest night of his life.

'Freddie! Freddie! Freddie!' the crowd chanted as he got into his manger's car. Some held up signs which read 'Go get him champ, spank the Yank.' Freddie loved the attention and waved to the crowd as he began the journey he hoped would end with him being crowned champion of the world.

On the surface, Freddie looked relaxed and happy as he peered out of the car window, but inside he felt a sense of foreboding. He felt a great responsibility to those people cheering and so badly wanted to win. The last time he felt like this was after the Len Harvey fight when he went AWOL from the RAF.

Once inside the dressing room, Mills felt no better. The noise from the fans outside felt distant. There was tension in the air.

As Nat Seller wrapped Freddie's hands, he kept reminding him to stick to the game plan.

'What do you think I am going to do, keep my hands down and let him pound me?' said Freddie half-jokingly.

Ignoring him, Seller kept on pressing the point, 'Get in first, make him take notice. Make sure you catch him. You miss and you are wide open for his big right.'

At the training camp, in front of the projector night after night, Freddie and Nat had carefully mapped out the game plan for the fight ahead. Lesnevich was proud of his right hand, which was rated the best in the world. Seller reasoned that Lesnevich would think Freddie would be wary of it. Therefore, in an effort to confuse him, Freddie would look to catch Lesnevich by surprise by wading in first.

The familiar buzzer rang, which told Freddie it was time to walk to the ring. Joining Seller was Ted Broadribb, who told his fighter, 'Whatever happens tonight, I am proud of you.' Freddie had his game face on and nodded his thanks.

Mills and Lesnevich instantly engaged with venom. Neither knew how to take a backward step and neither were afraid to mix it. The nerves Freddie felt in the dressing room vanished as he got down to work.

As expected, Lesnevich started fast, pushing Freddie to the ropes. In the first test of his game plan, Mills threw a series of right hooks to the head. Very soon, both boxers came together in a clinch. Once they were parted after the first ten seconds, Freddie got the first glimpse of his handiwork. A gash had opened up over Lesnevich's left eye.

A left hook met with even more success, ripping open a cut on the brow of the American's right eye. Things could not have started any better and all the way through Lesnevich would be plagued by cuts above his eyes.

While not in serious trouble, Lesnevich knew he could not afford to take too many punches and tried to clinch. Freddie followed up with series of body blows as he was determined to ensure the American knew he was in for a hard night.

As the bell rang to end the first round, Freddie went back to his corner satisfied with his work. Even though the left hook that opened up the cuts had wobbled Lesnevich, he was never in real danger. But that did not stop Freddie feeling he had taken the round.

From now on, it was about avoiding the dangerous right hand of the New Jersey native. At the start of the second Freddie carried on where he had left off, catching the incoming Lesnevich with another big right. The blow had little effect as the American went to work with his left, forcing Mills to cover up on occasions and keep out of range. The first heavy right hook from the American landed near the end of the round but the spoils were even.

During the interval, Freddie watched as Lesnevich's corner worked frantically to stem the bleeding from the cuts above his eyes. It was in stark contrast to their first encounter, when Freddie's corner tried desperately to revive their man after a disastrous second round.

As the blood flowed down Lesnevich's face at the start of the third, whatever treatment his corner had applied had failed as the cuts would just not close. But the American had not become world champion by lacking in guts and he rushed across the ring to launch an attack on Freddie, who responded with heavy punching to the mid-section. They then tied each other up before parting and keeping their distance.

The crowd was tiring of the caution showed by both fighters and began to get restless. Freddie knew his opponent was too dangerous to risk going at him all guns blazing. To win the world title, he had to stick to the game plan and stay out of range, whether the paying punters liked it or not. To most seasoned observers, the early rounds were scored as even.

Realising he was falling behind, Lesnevich sprang into action in the fourth. Before Freddie was properly off his stool,

Lesnevich was on him. But his cuts would not stop bleeding and his corner were concerned that they may force a stoppage.

The hours of film footage Mills had watched was paying off and he could tell that the man from New Jersey was trying to bring an early end to the bout. Lesnevich was becoming over-reliant on his famed right hand and Freddie was able to move out of the way, sliding along the ropes and using his left to stay out of danger. Freddie threw a few left hooks but Lesnevich still kept moving forward. At the end of the round, those at ringside felt Freddie just shaded it.

As the bell rang for the fifth round, it was clear that Lesnevich had changed tactics. Bouncing on his toes and flicking out his jab, he was trying to use lateral movement to frustrate Freddie into creating an opening.

During the rounds, Lesnevich's corner had been hard at work on the cuts and finally they stopped bleeding, clearing his vision. Both men swung wildly, missing with big left hooks, and Lesnevich was the first to score with a hard right to the body.

As the big puncher, Lesnevich was hoping to drag the Briton into a drawn-out, toe-to-toe battle. But Mills thought better of it and decided to retreat, yet Lesnevich was still able to use his left to good effect.

After the action in the fifth, Freddie was cautious in the sixth and seventh. Used to Mills' all-action style, the crowd began to get restless. They started slow hand-clapping and jeering as they demanded more action from the two men in the ring, who had both come with reputations as warriors.

Determined not to fall into the trap of over-confidence as he did in the first bout, Freddie blocked out the reaction of the audience. Apart from a hard right that caught him coming in and a right hook that caught Lesnevich off balance, the eighth and ninth rounds followed much the same pattern as the previous four.

The fight could be summed up in one moment as Lesnevich dashed out from his corner to meet Freddie with a right. For his part, Freddie went to the body before they fell into a clinch. The referee parted them only for the fighters to circle around each other slowly before one of them threw a punch, only for it to end in another clinch.

After one minute of the tenth round, the referee had seen enough. 'Come on, fellas, get stuck in. The crowd are about to riot if they don't see some action soon.' From this point on, the fight finally burst into life. Lesnevich connected with a hurtful left hook before Freddie hit back with a right hook that clumsily missed.

Quickly recovering his composure, Freddie threw a left that landed square on Lesnevich's jaw. He knew he had the American in trouble and this time he was not going to let him off the hook. Backing his man on to the ropes with several shots, the tough Lesnevich tried to weather the storm by working his way back on the inside with a right cross. But he was met with another vicious left hook from Freddie that put him on his hands and knees.

Eager to end it, Freddie advanced, his fists cocked and ready to administer the blows that would deliver him the world championship. Seeing the marauding British fighter on a mission, Lesnevich, summoning up all his years of experience, stayed on one knee, taking an eight count.

The extra seconds were meaningless as Lesnevich was still dazed and took another smashing left hook from the fists of Freddie. He went down again. Had Freddie not won the belt on points, what happened next might have been debated for years to come.

The count did not start until a couple of seconds after Lesnevich had hit the ground. To most people and those listening at home, Lesnevich had been counted out but the referee allowed him to continue.

Using every ounce of strength he could muster, Freddie threw a barrage of blows in a desperate attempt to finish it. But the man who had held the light-heavyweight title for seven years was not going to let go of his crown that easily.

As Freddie swung away, many of his blows hit the American's arms and shoulders. They looked good but had no effect.

When the bell rang for the end of the round, a disappointed and tired Mills trudged back to his corner.

From the 11th round onwards, it was clear that the Bournemouth man had missed his chance to put Lesnevich away. Even though Freddie continued to launch attacks to the body, they didn't carry the same ferocity or purpose and it quickly became clear that the previous round had sapped his energy.

Things got worse for Freddie in the 12th when the American firmly took control, using his left to drive Freddie back with his superior boxing skill. Even though Lesnevich's face was showing the effects of the relentless punching, it was Freddie who seemed to fade while his opponent was getting stronger all the time.

The fight had come alive and the crowd were roaring their approval. It was clear as the 13th round progressed that it would be a case of which fighter wanted to win the most. While Lesnevich looked the stronger of the two, he knew he was behind on points and was looking for the one punch that would end Freddie's valiant challenge.

It never came. Freddie swarmed all over the American, not allowing him to throw his right hand. Even when he did land with his famed right hook, it made no impact. There was drama at the end of the 14th when Lesnevich momentarily buckled Mills' legs just as the bell rang.

'Come on Freddie, this is anyone's fight. Knock him out and give the fans something to cheer,' Ted Broadribb shouted at Freddie as he sat on his stool preparing for the 15th and biggest round of his life. At the end of the next three minutes, Freddie would either be the first undisputed world champion from the British Isles in 45 years or just a footnote in boxing history.

As the bell rang, both men touched gloves. This might have been a boxing tradition but in this fight both combatants had gained a new-found respect for each other. To be sure of the win, Freddie had to put on the performance of a lifetime in the final round.

Freddie did not disappoint, giving everything. He put every last drop of energy into chasing the champion around the ring. Leading with his left, Freddie looked to chop down Lesnevich. To the capacity crowd, who were on their feet urging their hero to victory, there was only one winner. Lesnevich's face was a mess and he was looking like he had run out of ideas. Even his fabled right hand had absolutely no effect on Freddie.

Finally, after Freddie had punched himself to a standstill, the final bell rang. To those at White City and those listening on the radio, it was clear that Britain had a new world light-heavyweight champion.

There was a short interval before the result was declared. 'We've done it, Freddie, you're the champion of the world. We are going to make a pile of money now. America next stop for us,' Broadribb excitedly told his fighter at the end of the 15th.

The fight was a personal triumph for Freddie. He had faced up to Lesnevich's right hand, stayed out of trouble and not hit the canvas once. It was his best performance inside a boxing ring.

The referee did not give anything away. The master of ceremonies entered the ring and announced the scores. There was moment of silence across the arena as the crowd waited in anticipation for the verdict. Then it came. 'The winner of the bout... and the new light-heavyweight champion of the world, Fearless Freddie Mills!'

The crowd erupted into pandemonium. Broadribb and Seller embraced Mills, who lifted his hands above his head to acknowledge the roar of the crowd. It would take nearly an hour for Freddie to get out of the ring and back to the dressing room as he tried to work his way through the throng of fans.

It was an amazing achievement. Not since Cornishman Bob Fitzsimmons won the light-heavyweight championship by beating George Gardiner in November 1903 had anyone from the British Isles claimed that title. Even then, it could be argued that Fitzsimmons had left his native Cornwall for New Zealand at the age of nine. But there was a downside. Years later, Mills would say that he was in too much of a daze after the result was announced to enjoy the moment. He had little recollection of making his way back to the dressing room. At the moment of his greatest victory, he felt sick and dizzy.

Not that Freddie would have been able to get attention from medical staff even if he had wanted it. As he finally reached the dressing room, it was packed with celebrities and well-wishers eager to pat the new world champion on the back.

Life was never going to be same again for Freddie, who had cemented his status as a national treasure in the eyes of the British public. His name and face would be splashed across the front pages of every newspaper in the land.

It would take Freddie hours to get away from the former Olympic stadium that night. Mills and Broadribb struggled to get to the car as large swathes of the capacity crowd hung around long after the show ended to get an autograph. There was no doubt about it. At that precise moment, Freddie Mills was the biggest sporting superstar in Great Britain.

18

Chrissie and Don

WHEN they finally began the journey from White City back home, Ted Broadribb was in high spirits. 'We've agreed a return with Lesnevich at Madison Square Garden in September. Win that then the world is our oyster. Joe Louis will pack it in any day now. We will be well placed to go for the heavyweight title.'

As Broadribb waxed lyrical about dream fights with Ezzard Charles and Jersey Joe Walcott, Freddie was unable to focus. Broadribb might have been speaking fluent Cantonese for all he knew.

'Ted, you are going to have to stop the car. I am going to throw up.'

'What? Again?' This was the third time Broadribb had been forced to stop the car in a matter of miles.

Broadribb pulled into the nearest lay-by, where the new light-heavyweight champion of the world began retching.

Putting his arm around Freddie, Ted whispered to him, 'You better be well by the time we get back. Chrissie and Don have put a bit of a spread on for you.'

Chrissie and Don McCorkindale had become Freddie's closest friends. For years, Freddie was their lodger. They had all met in 1941, when Freddie joined Broadribb's stable of fighters. He had struck up a particularly close friendship with South African heavyweight Don.

They shared everything: boxing bills, rooms and eventually Don's wife Chrissie. However, Freddie was not returning to the room he rented from the McCorkindales but to a beautiful detached house in Denmark Hill, which he had a bought the previous year with Chrissie, who named it Joggi Villa.

Unbeknown to everyone except a few close friends, Chrissie McCorkindale had left her husband, taking her small son with her, to move in with Freddie.

Despite feeling the after-effects of a hard fight, Freddie could not let his friends down. As he walked through the door, he was smothered in kisses by a relieved Chrissie. Just behind stood her ex-husband, who waited in turn to give his best mate a huge hug.

Together with Ted, they sat down to talk about the future.

'Before you start on about the next match, Ted, there is only one match I am interested in right now,' Freddie interrupted. 'Chrissie, will you marry me?'

Instantly, she said 'yes', which was followed by more congratulations. Chief among these were Don's. He told Freddie, 'I hope you have more luck than I did with her,' before bursting into laughter.

Even before Freddie came along, the McCorkindales' marriage had been rocky. There had been money troubles with Don. Despite once owning a bar in Southwark, he was reduced to working on a building site. Chrissie had accused Don of demanding she indulge in unnatural acts, while Don had sued Chrissie in South Africa for the reinstatement of conjugal rights. The action was quickly dropped.

When Don finally discovered the affair with Freddie, rather than being annoyed at his friend's betrayal he was pleased his former wife and son would be looked after by his good friend. Don actively encouraged their relationship, allowing Chrissie to divorce him on the grounds of his unreasonable behaviour.

That was all in the past now. Freddie climbed into bed with Chrissie a world champion and newly engaged. It seemed like his life was on the up and up.

The following morning, Chrissie struggled to raise him from a deep sleep. When he did wake up, Freddie acted like he had suffered a stroke. One side of his face was numb and he slurred his speech so much that those around him struggled to understand what he said.

After being called by a worried Chrissie, Ted Broadribb was waiting in the lounge of Joggi Villa by the time Freddie came downstairs after another deep sleep.

'Freddie, I want you to go and see a specialist. You have not been right for months,' Broadribb said.

A visit to a different Harley Street specialist was arranged. Over the course of a few hours, Freddie had a battery of tests. The results of the X-rays were even worse than they were before the Lesnevich fight.

In front of both Ted and Chrissie, the doctor gave Freddie his diagnosis. 'The news is not good, I'm afraid. The X-ray has revealed the displacement of five vertebrae in your spine. The symptoms you have been experiencing are as a result of multiple concussions. The slurred speech points to the early signs of being punch drunk.'

The Harley Street specialist's advice was devastating. 'Mr. Mills, if you do not want to end your days in a wheelchair or as a vegetable, I strongly advise you undergo an operation and retire from the ring. Simply put, you cannot risk taking any more punches to the head.'

All three politely thanked the doctor and made their way out.

'Yeah, perhaps you should have a rest?' Ted suggested. 'You know, take two to three months off.'

The Sunday papers shocked Freddie. Someone had got wind of the diagnoses from Harley Street and claimed he would never be seen in a ring again. They informed readers that the beating from Lesnevich was so bad, doctors had advised him not to fight again.

In response, Ted Broadribb issued a statement telling journalists that Freddie was going to take a rest for a few months so he could focus on his personal life.

Despite being one of the most famous men in Great Britain, Freddie's private life was shrouded in mystery. There was no girlfriend to talk of and he had never brought anyone home to meet his mother. His whole life had been dedicated to his sport.

Therefore, journalists at the offices of the *News Chronicle* were shocked when they were tipped off that Freddie was to marry at a small Methodist Chapel on Herne Hill on 30 September 1948. To the newsmen, it seemed a strange choice. Chrissie was five years older than Freddie, had recently been divorced and had a young son.

Like the rest of their relationship, the wedding was so secret that Freddie's mother Lottie only found out when a reporter from the *Bournemouth Echo* knocked on her door the following day asking her to comment. She simply shrugged her shoulders and shook her head.

To any casual observer, Chrissie had become the new mother figure in Freddie's life. For the rest of his days, both in public and private, he would call his new wife 'mummy'. Chrissie even described Freddie as an overgrown child who loved nothing more than having his head cuddled by the fire.

There was no time for a honeymoon. Ted Broadribb had arranged for Freddie to fly to Johannesburg to take on heavyweight Johnny Ralph. Accompanying him with Broadribb was sparring partner Johnny Williams, who also fought on the bill and roomed with Freddie, and Chrissie's ex-husband Don McCorkindale.

For flying to South Africa, Freddie was handsomely paid, the equivalent of £55,000 today. Johnny Ralph was seen as a rising star. He was unbeaten and held wins over two of Freddie's former opponents, Stephane Olek and Ken Shaw. At 23, he was six years younger than Freddie.

From the moment Freddie stepped off the plane, he was the talk of the town. Ever the cheeky chappie, he always seemed to have a quick one-liner for the press. To promote the fight, he appeared at the old Plaza Theatre in Johannesburg, going through a familiar routine that included demonstrating his boxing skills while telling jokes and stories.

Remembering the problems he had with the heat on his last visit, Freddie spent a few weeks acclimatising to the weather. After an enjoyable training camp that included sparring with McCorkindale, Freddie entered the Wembley Stadium in Johannesburg oozing the type of confidence only champions exude. He walked to the ring smiling and waving at the crowd.

As Freddie entered the ring, he could be forgiven for thinking he was back home in Britain as the 26,000-strong audience roared their approval for the world light-heavyweight champion.

Ralph, who was still quite early into his career, outweighed Freddie by 16lb but was tense. At the first bell, despite his visible nervousness, it was Ralph who started the more confident of the two. Bouncing on the balls of his feet, he began flicking out the jab. A straight left snapped Mills' head back but did not seem to trouble the British fighter.

Ralph had a very nice left and he scored quite freely during rounds one and two, but landed nothing in particular to bother Freddie. None of the punches Ralph threw remotely compared with the sledgehammer-like blows he had received in his last fight with Lesnevich.

When the second round started, Freddie began to work the body, pushing Ralph back and cutting off the ring. A few good right hooks seemed to sap the confidence of the South African. Remembering the problems he had had with the altitude in South Africa on previous occasions, Freddie was careful to control his breathing.

The gulf in experience between world champion and tentative novice was beginning to tell in the fourth round. With chopping rights, Freddie was firmly in control, catching Ralph at will while his opponent offered little in return.

In the last minute of the fifth, a totally dominant Freddie threw a flurry of punches in search of the one shot to put Ralph on his back. However, a right hand from Ralph on the bell momentarily dazed Mills.

Not that anyone watching would have noticed as Freddie tore out of his corner for the sixth. With two-fisted aggression he went to work, mixing up shots to head and the body, and really started to hurt Ralph. After half a minute of intense pressure that saw Ralph cover up with his back pressed against the ropes, a short left sent him down for a count of eight.

As he quickly tried to come to his senses, another shot saw him down for a count of three. He sank to the canvas three more times but was saved by the bell. It could, however, be argued that all three of the knockdowns came from illegal punches that landed around the back of the head, so-called 'rabbit' punches.

Despite hanging on for dear life in the sixth, the big South African staged something of a comeback in the seventh in what was a relatively quiet round for Freddie, although Ralph's punches had very little power behind them. Freddie had put so much into the previous round that he had to take things more easily to conserve energy. Despite being in trouble in the sixth, Ralph took the bout into the eighth round.

The end came when Freddie backed up his opponent and dropped him with a short right. Freddie's rest had done him good and he went on to finish this round quickly. After some heavy body blows, he landed two left hooks and then the finishing shot that put Ralph out for the count after just 45 seconds. It was the first time in Ralph's fledging career that he had been knocked out. Freddie sportingly helped the South African to his feet.

If Mills was satisfied with his evening's work, the local press were not, citing the illegal punches Freddie threw in the sixth round. There was also criticism of the referee and claims that he was in a hurry to count out Ralph. It was argued that the fight film showed the referee counting two or three seconds before Freddie had walked to the side of the ring, not to a neutral corner as stipulated in the rules.

Not that any of the negative press reaction worried Mills. The only concern at the end of the fight was that he lost his footing in the ring on three occasions.

Amongst the congratulatory telegrams from well-wishers was a letter from the Consolidated Theatres of South Africa, who were so impressed with Freddie's star turn at the Plaza Theatre that they offered him a fortnight's engagement on the stage. The first week was to be in Cape Town and the second in Durban. The money was too good to miss, so Freddie delayed his plans to return home to resurrect his act in two of South Africa's biggest cities.

While happy to return home to his new life in Great Britain, Freddie had fallen in love with South Africa and wanted to take his new bride to the country. In January 1949, Freddie and Chrissie flew out to the African continent. Accompanying them on the trip was Chrissie's son Don Jr and his father Don McCorkindale.

On arrival at the Plaza Hotel, Cape Town, the trio booked into two rooms, with Don sharing with his young son and Freddie and Chrissie in the room below. To all the world, they seemed like three friends holidaying together. Little did anyone suspect that the two men had been married to the same woman and she was enjoying her honeymoon with a new husband.

If anyone knew the arrangement, things would have seemed stranger still when husband number one frolicked with husband number two in the pool. Old cine camera footage taken by Chrissie shows Don hoisting Freddie on his shoulders before playfully throwing him into the hotel pool. Later, they are seen splashing water at each other. Years later, Chrissie would describe them as an oddity.

Since Freddie's death, there has been speculation about the true nature of Freddie's relationship with the McCorkindales. Certainly, Don McCorkindale's reaction to his wife leaving him for his best friend was bizarre. There are theories which suggest Don McCorkindale was the real object of Freddie's affections, although this was based on the anecdotes of others and not any hard evidence, which casts doubt on the truth of these stories.

What is certain is that Freddie was a family man and devoted to his two daughters Susan and Amanda, as well as his adopted son Don Jr. A few years later, Don McCorkindale returned to South Africa, where he saw out his days as a cinema manager before dying in August 1970, a few days shy of his 66th birthday.

Over the years, Freddie's marriage and subsequent honeymoon would be a strange incident in the increasingly bizarre life he was beginning to lead.

19

This time next year

EARLY in March 1949, an air of excitement surrounded the offices of promoter Jack Solomons. The foremost fight fixer in Great Britain lit a cigar, leaned back in his chair and for the umpteenth time read the telegram in his hands. It announced that after 12 years as the heavyweight champion of the world, Joe Louis was retiring from the ring.

Solomons had been planning for this moment for months. There had been rumours from the Louis camp that he was planning to walk away after his last defence against Jersey Joe Walcott. The wily promoter had already reached an agreement with the British Boxing Board of Control that they would recognise a fighter promoted by Solomons as the world heavyweight champion.

Now with Louis' retirement, he could set the wheels in motion. The two most popular fighters in Britain were Freddie Mills and Bruce Woodcock. Having just one on the bill was a guaranteed sell-out. Solomons closed his eyes and could almost hear the roar of the crowd as Woodcock from the North and Freddie from the South battled it out for the opportunity to fight for the world heavyweight championship.

Waiting for the winner was American Lee Savold, who had already lost to Woodcock by disqualification in 1944. If Freddie or Woodcock could get past Savold and claim a portion of the world title, then Solomons would be in a strong position to negotiate a bout with either Ezzard Charles or Jersey Joe Walcott, who were to battle for the crown vacated by Louis.

The plan had worked before. He had enticed Gus Lesnevich to come over and put his title on the line against Freddie in 1946 by claiming the Bournemouth man held the British portion of the world title after knocking out Len Harvey.

As Solomons picked up the phone to call Ted Broadribb, he could picture a sold-out Wembley Stadium hosting a world heavyweight title fight involving a British fighter, with him as promoter. It was his dream and now he felt he was only months away from making it a reality.

Everything was in place. Both Broadribb and Tommy Hurst, who handled the affairs of Bruce Woodcock, had privately agreed to the fight in the event of Louis' retirement. The only sticking point was Freddie, who still hoped for a return with Lesnevich at Madison Square Garden.

It was an animated Broadribb who had driven round to Joggi Villa after putting the phone down on Jack Solomons an hour earlier. Walking around the garden, Broadribb tried to convince Freddie that taking on Woodcock in a rematch made perfect sense.

'Freddie Mills, the heavyweight champion of the world, has a certain ring to it. It's what you've dreamed of since you first laced up a pair of gloves.'

'Ted, I'm the best *light-heavy* in the world. Why would I need Bruce?'

'It would be the biggest fight in Britain. Bruce's British, European and Empire titles on the line. You would walk through Savold. Just imagine headlining Madison Square Garden as the heavyweight champion of the world. Freddie paced from one end of the garden to the other, deep in thought. Finally, after being convinced by Broadribb that if he got past Woodcock and Savold he could beat either Ezzard Charles, who his manager labelled a blown-up middleweight, or Jersey Joe Walcott, who was an 'old man', Freddie agreed to the fight.

Broadribb nodded his agreement. He was confident Freddie would overcome Woodcock. Mills had looked like a man reborn against Lesnevich and Ralph. On the other hand, Woodcock's career looked to be going in the opposite direction. He had suffered a detached retina that left him blind in one eye against Joe Baksi and was forced to retire after his knee gave way against top contender Tami Mauriello.

Light training for the biggest fight between two British fighters since Len Harvey and Jock McAvoy faced off just over a decade earlier began at Brixton. Among the crowd of youngsters were two boxing-mad brothers, Ronnie and Reggie Kray, who watched in awe as their idol was put through his paces by Nat Seller.

As preparations got more serious, Freddie moved out to Betchworth, a Surrey village with which he was familiar. Unlike his previous camp there before the Lesnevich fight, things went well. His sparring partners Johnny Williams and Ken Shaw had never seen Freddie more confident or determined. The headaches had subsided and a daily massage eased the pain in his neck and shoulders.

Each day ended at a local pub, the Barley Mow, where Seller would convince Freddie that Woodcock was on the slide and not the same man he had faced nearly three years earlier. As they wound down training, Seller was so confident that he predicted an early stoppage for Mills.

'Hello fellas,' said a cheerful Freddie as he addressed the assembled press at Jack Solomons' gymnasium at Old Compton Street for the weigh-in on the morning of 2 June 1949. The hype was at fever pitch and all week the newspapers and radio had been covering the fight. Such was the interest, the press and public had queued to get into the small building just off Piccadilly for hours.

Many were still camped outside as the light-heavyweight champion of the world burst into song, 'There's no business like the fight business like no business I know!' A wide grin spread across Freddie's face as Woodcock entered the room. 'Ah Bruce! There was me thinking you wasn't going to turn up.'

'There I was thinking the same thing,' the charismatic Yorkshireman replied as he shook Freddie's hand. Both were acting like old friends meeting for a drink rather than two men who in a few short hours would be trading blows in the ring.

As they stood together, there did not seem to be that much difference in size, with Woodcock slightly the taller man at 6ft to Freddie's 5ft 10in. But the scales told a different story, with Woodcock weighing 20 pounds heavier.

As they climbed down from the temporary stage set up especially for the weigh-in, a reporter from the BBC stuck a microphone in Freddie's face, 'Hello to all sports fans and particularly to those back home in Bournemouth. I am in good shape for this fight,' Freddie told the listeners.

When asked for a prediction, before Freddie could answer someone behind him shouted, 'He'll bleedin' murder him, take his head off!' Freddie laughed and replied, 'Who am I to argue with that?'

As Freddie headed back to his manager's house, Broadribb was supremely confident. 'He's scared. Tommy Hurst said he's been shitting himself all week. He nearly didn't turn up today.'

'Yeah, he looked a little flabby around the middle. First chance I get, I am going to take him out. I deserve an early night for once,' replied Freddie, unusually self-assured.

Such was Freddie's fame, a police escort to the arena had become a common occurrence. If anything, Freddie was sure the crowds that lined the streets on the way to the White City Stadium were twice the size of those that had turned out when he faced Lesnevich just a year earlier.

In his mind he ran through, over and over again, what he was going to do to Woodcock. Get stuck in early, move to the right so he could not see the punches coming. He was going to show his appreciation for the fans by delivering a spectacular knockout. He had not felt this good in years. The fight could not come soon enough.

The hundreds who waited in anticipation for the weigh-in were only a taster for the 46,000 who had crammed into the old Olympic stadium to see Mills and Woodcock battle it out in the ring.

The night had got off to a great start. Just as Freddie arrived at the arena, he was met by sparring partner Johnny Williams, who had just pulled off a big win against Sweden's Nisse Anderson. Ever superstitious, Freddie took this as a lucky omen.

Just as Freddie finished loosening up, there was a knock on the door. It was Jack Solomons informing him the crowd were ready for their first look at the light-heavyweight champion of the world. 'I just saw Bruce, he's not looking good, Freddie. Go easy on him.'

'Fuck that, I am going to send a message to Lee Savold and anybody else who wants it.'

As Freddie walked to the ring, he could feel the crackle of anticipation and excitement in the air. He stepped through the ropes and took a look at Woodcock. As the referee pulled them together for their final instructions, Freddie's stare almost pierced through his opponent, who looked away. Gone was the friendliness of a few hours ago as both returned to their corners in anticipation of the first bell.

The first round began and Freddie was as good as his word to Broadribb, launching himself at Woodcock and looking to take the Doncaster fighter out early. Anticipating a fast start from Mills, Woodcock met the onslaught with three powerful rights to the jaw. Halfway through the first round, Mills saw an opening and threw a big left hook but it had no effect on the bigger man. Using his weight advantage, Woodcock clinched Mills, smothering his attack.

Woodcock was using his left efficiently to fend off any attack. Another clinch and Mills found himself in trouble. A right caught him flush on the chin while a left over the right eye pushed him back to the ropes.

Holding his hands high above his head, Mills bobbed and weaved, trying to stay away from the quick fists of Woodcock. When that did not work he decided to fight fire with fire, launching a two-handed attack on the Doncaster man.

It was a huge error and a straight right caught the incoming Mills on the side of the head. The Bournemouth fighter was hurt. Freddie then took a thunderous right that landed square on his chin and he was on his knees receiving a count for the first time since the Lloyd Marshall fight some two years before.

He jumped back up just as the referee reached the count of two. Getting up too soon after a knockdown was a mistake Mills had made repeatedly throughout his career and it was not long before Woodcock was swarming all over the lighter man, looking to end proceedings in the first round. However, a lunging left at the end of the round showed the crowd Mills was still in the fight.

As he sat on his stool, Freddie knew he had lost the first round and still felt groggy from the knockdown. Far from being a shot fighter, Woodcock looked the sharper and faster of the two. 'That's all he's got, he will run out of steam. You've weathered the storm, Freddie,' Seller reassured him.

Freddie came out for the second determined to make an impression on the fight. Woodcock responded to a body attack from Mills with an attempted straight left. This time Freddie was wise to it and ducked under the jab as he continued to work the body.

It was clear Freddie hoped that by working the body hard, the head would inevitably follow. The tactic seemed to be working and a huge left hook hurt Woodcock, his legs buckling temporarily. Throughout the round, Mills mixed up his work to head and body. That is not to say Woodcock took this willingly, throwing a few solid punches of his own, although a good right to the jaw staggered the bigger man as Freddie evened the score in rounds.

Freddie was determined to end the bout early and a huge right hook that landed squarely on Woodcock's jaw made his opponent aware of his intentions. The second round had convinced him that Nat Seller was right. To the overconfident Mills, it was only a matter of time before he dropped Woodcock.

Buoyed by his early success, Freddie got carried away, leaving himself wide open with an attempted overhand right. The reckless swing was met with a painful short right from Woodcock, dropping Freddie to his knees for a count of four. The pendulum had swung in favour of the Yorkshireman as Woodcock threw a barrage with both fists.

The eye that had troubled Freddie in their first meeting began to swell again. When he did manage to get in some shots of his own, he was met by Woodcock's ramrod straight left. A huge right from Woodcock shook Freddie again before the session was over. Freddie was hanging on for dear life.

It was the same eye that had been damaged by Lloyd Marshall and Freddie went back to his corner in some pain. 'Work the body, work the body,' Nat Seller urged as he frantically tried to get the swelling down on Freddie's damaged eye.

A missed right hook from Woodcock in the fourth gave Freddie the opportunity to follow Seller's advice and viciously attack the body. Having trouble with his own eyesight, Woodcock kept missing. A few crisp jabs from Freddie and the bigger man's nose was broken. Mills was back in the fight but was frustrated every time he tried to launch an attack by the Doncaster man's effective straight left.

By the fifth, Woodcock was missing so much that he was beginning to look clumsy. A left to the body and a wicked right hand from Mills had him looking worried. Freddie continued jabbing with his own left, making Woodcock's nose bleed profusely. By the time the bell rang for the interval, it looked as though, slowly but surely, Freddie was beginning to turn the tide. He was confident he had taken the last two rounds on the scorecards.

If Woodcock was shaken up by the events of the previous round, he did not show it and began the sixth by throwing two massive right hooks at the smaller man. However, the Doncaster fighter went to the well one too many times. Attempting the trick again, he swung at Mills, missed and slipped.

From that moment on, many of the press men watching the fight just below the ropes were surprised at how easily Freddie found it to penetrate Woodcock's defence with his left jab. Throughout the round, the blood from Woodcock's nose turned from a trickle into a heavy bleed.

The seventh saw the fight descend into a see-saw battle. After another ferocious attack to Woodcock's body, Freddie walked into a big right hand on the chin. Both combatants then got into an exchange that saw heavy punches thrown. In this round, Mills stayed on the back foot, although he threw a few good punches, and he had to fight his way off the ropes as Woodcock ended the round strongly.

For the third time in the fight, Freddie was on the canvas in the eighth. Things had begun well enough with a strong body attack then some good work behind the left jab. However, the timing that had been missing from Woodcock's work in the fifth and sixth finally returned, with two pitch-perfect right hands putting Mills down for a count of two.

The rest of the round was merely about survival for Freddie as Woodcock punished his smaller opponent with heavy rights that connected to head and body. The only positive was the volley of punches Freddie managed in the closing stages.

For most observers, Woodcock was firmly on top but that did not mean Mills was incapable of springing a surprise. A left and right to the body from Woodcock early in the ninth saw Freddie respond in kind with two better shots of his own. Two big right hands that landed on the jaw saw Woodcock fire back, but it was Freddie's left that was causing the damage as Woodcock continued to bleed heavily from the nose.

By the tenth, it seemed as if Mills was beginning to tire and an early attack to the body quickly petered out. Woodcock threw a right hook that seemed to take all the energy out of Freddie.

A rapid left-right combination to the head sent Mills to the canvas for the fourth time in the fight. Sensibly, he took to his knee and was up at the count of nine. The short breather gave him renewed vigour as he launched himself at Woodcock, but it was all in vain as he took some more heavy shots before the round was out.

After each knockdown, Freddie seemed to perform stronger in the following round. This was the case in the 11th, when he focused on body punching. Woodcock was also tiring, visibly slowing down and looking to measure his opponent with his left in the hope of throwing a big right hook. More often than not, Freddie and Woodcock stood toe to toe, both looking for the one shot to end it all.

It was clear by the 12th that Freddie was all out of energy and fighting on instinct. The first real skirmish of the round saw Mills on the floor again. The punch that sent him there looked innocuous enough but his tired legs would not hold him up. The referee looked at Freddie with serious concern after he got up at three and was trapped on the ropes, not throwing anything in return.

Halfway through the round, Freddie dug deep and threw a left, hurting his opponent and damaging Woodcock's nose once again. However, by the end of the round Woodcock was landing at will on the tiring Mills. Based on this round, onlookers felt the end could not be far away.

In the 13th, a desperate Freddie was wild, throwing anything, hoping to catch Woodcock with the one punch that would score him a knockout. It never came and Woodcock bossed the ring, peppering Mills with both hands.

A strong right eventually put Freddie down for a two-count. Sensing the fight was going out of him, he launched himself at Woodcock once back on his feet. He was down again but back up before the referee could begin the count.

By the end of the round, Freddie was throwing haymakers but they only connected with thin air, as any chance of being crowned the British, European and Empire champion slipped away.

Freddie's final assault in the 14th lacked any kind of conviction. It was clear that the Bournemouth fighter had nothing left in the tank. Woodcock clinically waited his chance, which came with three efficient rights to his opponent's head. Freddie had had enough and sank down to one knee, looking at the referee as he counted him out.

Once the referee reached the count of ten, Freddie rose to his feet and walked slowly to his corner, holding the back of his neck. The pain was just too much and if Mills did not know it beforehand he could ill afford to take that type of punishment from anyone, let alone the British, European and Empire heavyweight champion, for much longer.

To make matters worse, Mills began vomiting before he even left the ring.

He only made it back to the dressing room with the help of Johnny Williams. Inside, he was helped on to the rub-down table as Broadribb tried in vain to keep the press from entering.

Unable to move, he partially opened his eyes and asked Seller what had happened.

'You did well Freddie, you did well.'

They were the last words Freddie heard before losing consciousness. It took nearly an hour to rouse him and even more time to get him dressed. The trip home was horrendous, with Broadribb having to stop regularly to allow Freddie to throw up. For days afterwards, he could not look into light or speak without slurring.

Not that Freddie would have any recollection of this. Later, he would say he had an out-of-body experience in the 12th round and the only thing he could remember was someone mumbling to him between the 13th and 14th. It was clear that Freddie was suffering from another concussion, made worse by the displaced vertebrae in his neck. He would not fight again during 1949.

For his part, Woodcock was indeed matched with Lee Savold for the vacant championship, as recognised by the British Boxing Board of Control, at White City in June 1950. No one outside Great Britain thought it was a title fight but none of that worried the crowd of more than 50,000.

Woodcock was beaten in four rounds but he fought once more, losing his British, European and Commonwealth titles to Jack Gardener. He then retired to run a pub in his native Doncaster. For Freddie, the dream of winning the world heavyweight crown had come to an end but he was still a world champion and the British public had not seen the last of him in the boxing ring.

20

Maxed out

AFTER the Woodcock fight, Ted Broadribb told Freddie to go away and enjoy married life with Chrissie. They agreed to talk about Freddie's future after he returned from holiday in Devon. After a hectic couple of years, Broadribb was enjoying some peace and quiet away from the fight game.

That peace was broken one August morning by a loud banging on his front door. Sitting in his pyjamas enjoying breakfast, Ted quickly put on some slippers and his dressing gown to see what all the commotion was about.

Once he opened the door, Broadribb was confronted by an angry Freddie Mills. Barging his way past his manager, Mills stormed into Broadribb's front room. 'You got some serious explaining to do,' Freddie fumed as he thrust two pieces of paper into Broadribb's face.

After fumbling around for his glasses, Broadribb read the letters Freddie had received at Joggi Villa upon his return from holiday.

The first had been sent by air mail, direct from New York City. It was from the National Boxing Association, which recognised Mills as world light-heavyweight champion.

The letter asked Freddie, in light of the fact he had not defended the crown in the year since he won it, whether he intended to relinquish the belt. Furthermore, if he wished to remain recognised as champion he had 90 days to arrange a fight with number one contender Joey Maxim or be stripped of the title.

'Nothing to worry about, Freddie. Jack will sort it,' replied Broadribb nonchalantly. Freddie would not be pacified and furiously urged his manager to read the other piece of paper.

Quickly, Broadribb unfolded another letter, this one far more formal in tone. It informed Freddie his Majesty's Customs and Excises had found he had failed to pay tax on his earnings since leaving the Royal Air Force in 1946. According to their calculations, Freddie owed nearly £5,000. The sum had to be paid in full within three months or action would be taken to recover it.

It was true that Broadribb had not paid a penny in tax since Freddie agreed to fight Lesnevich in 1946. It never occurred to him to employ an accountant even when Freddie was earning some of the biggest purses in his career. Stuttering, he blurted out the first thing that came into his head, 'You will have to come to some sort of arrangement with them.'

What made Freddie even angrier was that when he queried why he was only receiving small amounts from the huge purses he earned, Ted informed him a large chunk of the money had been gobbled up by the taxman. 'If the money hasn't gone on tax, where the fuck's it gone, Ted? You've ripped me off.'

For over an hour, Freddie ranted and raved at Broadribb, labelling him a 'spiv', a 'conman' and a 'thief'. At one point, Ted was concerned Freddie had gotten so mad that he was about to hit him.

Finally, Broadribb said he would talk to Jack Solomons. Promising a quick solution to the problems, Freddie finally left his father-in-law's house. Within minutes, Broadribb was on the phone to Britain's premier promoter. 'Jack, you are going to have to sort this. Freddie will kill me if you don't.'

Reassuring Broadribb that he was close friends with Jack 'Doc' Kearns, who was the official matchmaker for the National Boxing Association, Solomons was confident he could persuade the executive to waive their ruling.

On the tax bill, Solomons told Broadribb he had two options: either sell Freddie's contract to another manager or convince him to fight Joey Maxim. Of the two, Broadribb's preference was for Freddie to fight Maxim. He was sure the receipts from the bout would enable him to wipe the slate clean with the taxman.

When confronted with the options, Freddie was unhappy. He worried about losing Joggi Villa and his businesses, which included a transport café, a Chinese restaurant and a few small houses that provided rental income. Everything he had worked so hard for was on the line. Rather than agreeing to fight Maxim, he wanted Broadribb to try and sell his contract.

An idyllic summer began to turn into a nightmare autumn for Freddie. Despite Broadribb's best efforts, he could not sell Freddie's contract. The only firm proposal received was from an American who offered £1,250, which was nowhere near enough.

By October, both Broadribb and Mills had run out of options. Things had become desperate. Without the knowledge of his wife, Freddie was contemplating selling his beloved Joggi Villa. This eventuality was unacceptable to Freddie, meaning he had to bow to the inevitable. He would have to step through the ropes once again. Within a matter of days, Jack Solomons had reached an agreement with Doc Kearns for Freddie to face off against Joey Maxim at Earl's Court on 24 January 1950.

Joey Maxim, who was born Giuseppe Antonio Berardinelli, was a veteran of 87 fights and at 28 was only two years younger than Freddie. He had earned his shot at the title by winning a unanimous decision over Gus Lesnevich after 15 brutal rounds in 1949.

Never seen as a heavy hitter, what Maxim lacked in power he more than made up for with technical skill. Beginning his professional career in 1941 at the age of 18, he had only knocked out nine of his previous opponents and was firmly rated the underdog when he signed to fight Mills.

As Freddie put pen to paper for a fight he did not want, he felt he had been led up the garden path by Broadribb. The promises of a rematch with Lesnevich in Madison Square Garden had failed to materialise. He was talked into a fight with Woodcock and now was facing a massive tax bill, which had only been paid thanks to a large advance from Jack Solomons for the Maxim fight.

It was an aggrieved Freddie who kissed Chrissie goodbye in November to travel to Betchworth to begin serious training. Freddie's mood did not improve when Nat Seller told him on arrival that the weather was so cold it would not be possible to set up a ring outside, as had been the practice in the past. Instead, he would train in the public bar of the Barley Mow.

At the same time, the papers told Freddie that his opponent would be enjoying state-of-the-art facilities at Jack Solomons' gymnasium in Windmill Street. Things came to a head one day when Freddie was shadow boxing while being overseen by Nat Seller.

'You're not trying, Freddie, make an effort.'

Freddie could not hold his temper any longer. 'This is a joke, no ring, no sparring, and it's a waste of time. Why are you here, Nat? Fuck off. I don't want you around no more.'

Seller smiled. He had heard it before but this time Freddie was menacing. 'You better fuck off now, Nat, before I clock you one.' It was not the first time in this camp that Mills had threatened Seller with violence. He knew Freddie was serious and that night was on the train back to London, where he landed at Broadribb's door.

'I am telling you, Ted, he's lost it. The other night, he threatened some bloke in the bar for spilling his pint. A few days ago, I held the pads up for him and he hit me in the face and never apologised.'

Seller went on, 'Johnny Williams tells me he is wild in sparring. He's like a bear with a sore head.'

It would take Broadribb, who did not travel down to Surrey, a full three days to persuade Freddie over the phone to take Seller back. Even then, Freddie would refuse to speak to his trainer directly when he returned to the camp.

The bravado Freddie had displayed at the weigh-in with Bruce Woodcock was gone. He just wanted to get the fight out of the way. Knowing Maxim had been knocked out early in his career after only 51 seconds, Freddie hoped to catch the Cleveland native cold. The press were looking beyond the fight, with rumours that Sugar Ray Robinson wanted to take on the winner in an attempt to win world titles at three different weights.

For the third consecutive fight, Mills arrived at Earl's Court by police escort. The crowd was way down on the 46,000 who had come to see him battle it out with Bruce

Woodcock, but the venue was still sold out, with many tickets fetching as much as five times their face value on the black market.

There was tension in the dressing room before the fight. The relationship between Freddie and Seller had deteriorated to the point where Mills would not allow his trainer to wrap his hands, asking his masseur Frank Duffet to do it instead. Perhaps it was nerves but just 20 minutes before he was called out for his walk to the ring, Freddie had his head down the toilet being violently sick.

'Ted, he's throwing up in there,' Seller informed the manager. 'Just leave him, Nat,' replied Broadribb.

As the buzzer sounded for Freddie to emerge from his dressing room, there were no words of encouragement from Broadribb or Solomons.

A fanfare greeted both boxers. The crowd were shrouded in darkness as the spotlights were turned to show the two fighters stripped to the waist, awaiting the bell to signal the start of the first round. Mills looked solid, his face taut. He waited impatiently, ready to tear into his American challenger.

Across the ring, Maxim looked focused and determined. He had watched film reels of Mills' fights and knew Freddie's game plan better than his own. An intelligent fighter, he would use his speed and accurate left jab to keep off the marauding Mills. That way, he hoped to build up a commanding points lead.

Over and over, Freddie reminded himself, Maxim had lost in a first-round knockout to Curtis Shepherd after only 51 seconds. He told himself this boy was nothing but a light hitter with a suspect chin. It was going to be an easy night. How wrong he was.

The sound of the first bell was like a red rag to a bull for Freddie, who started quickly, looking to impose himself. A huge left hook to the body and a wild overhand right connected, driving the American to the ropes.

Believing he had Maxim in trouble, Freddie looked to finish the fight early. In a moment of high drama the American hung on, crowding out Mills and stopping him from landing any more damaging punches. The referee broke them apart. As soon as there was some space, Mills closed it with a few heavy left hooks that shook Maxim.

As the bell rang to end the round, Freddie walked to the corner believing he had taken the round. Confident his best shots had managed to hurt the American, he was sure he was going to walk through Maxim in the second.

The bell rang and again Freddie rushed Maxim, pushing him back towards the ropes. A good left on the jaw once again shook him and Freddie went in for the kill. At this point, the only tactic Maxim could employ effectively was to clinch and smother Freddie's in-fighting.

As they broke from another clinch, Maxim finally got in a shot of his own, with a left hook to the Briton's face momentarily appearing to stop him in his tracks. Freddie responded with two-fisted aggression. Showing flashes of his boxing skill, Maxim threw two good combinations that kept the prowling Mills at bay.

As the session came to a close, Freddie felt disappointed he had failed to end the fight. However, each time he got in close Maxim hung on, although press observers would later say excessively.

It was clear to the American's corner that some of Freddie's biggest punches had the power to hurt their man. As the bell rang for the third round, Mills was confident that he was still in for an early night.

The third round found Freddie in an assertive mood. Until this round, apart from a few flurries, Maxim had seemed wary of Freddie's power and unwilling to engage. The British champion went to work on the body of the American. Yet again, Maxim clung on for dear life. A warning was issued to both fighters halfway through the round for refusing to break.

After they had been pulled apart by the referee, Maxim delivered an exquisite left uppercut that hurt the champion, leaving him in a daze for the rest of the round. It was Freddie's turn to hang on as Maxim looked to press home his advantage. A left hook that hurt Maxim subdued the attack as both fighters went back to clinching, prompting more warnings from the referee.

Despite being stunned, all was not lost for Freddie. Maxim had been hurt while his habit of clinching gave Freddie belief his opponent could not handle inside work. In the opposite corner, Maxim knew he had to change tactics. He had been surprised by the strength of Mills and had not stuck to his game plan. As both fighters stood up in readiness, something had to change.

A more stylish Maxim emerged for the fourth round. Circling Mills, he began throwing out his left jab, peppering his opponent's face every time he came in close, although this did not mean Freddie was unsuccessful with his big shots. A big right hand landed, causing blood to trickle down the left cheek of the Cleveland man.

This time, instead of going for the clinch, as he had done in previous rounds, Maxim responded with a string of combinations. Many of the punches hit Freddie on the arms and gloves, but the speed of the shots meant others got through. They hurt Freddie, who was struggling from the beginning of the round to deal with the accurate left jab that Maxim kept pumping in his face.

It was clear as both fighters took their obligatory one-minute rest that Maxim had just had his best round of the fight. Each punch he landed had stung and little did he know but Freddie was beginning to feel dizzy. The speed at which Maxim was throwing meant it was difficult for Mills to throw anything of note back. The Bournemouth fighter knew he had to think of something fast.

Freddie began to rely on brute force, knowing there was no way he could take much more of the punishment that Maxim had dished out in the previous round. Once again rushing the American, his wild punches disorientated the challenger. At one stage, it did look as though the full-on attack would finally put Maxim on the floor.

As Freddie swarmed all over Maxim, looking to end things, the American had one thing in his arsenal he knew could trouble the Brit. It was not long before Maxim used it, firing a huge left hook that ended a high-octane assault. For the first time in the bout, Freddie looked in trouble and suddenly it was Maxim throwing lefts and rights, trapping his opponent in the corner.

As Freddie moved away along the ropes, Maxim followed him, handing out a real beating, worrying spectators for a moment that the world light-heavyweight championship was about to be taken across the Atlantic. Summoning up all his courage, Freddie came back in the only way he knew how, throwing punches that deterred Maxim from continuing his attack.

While the earlier work from Freddie saw him take the round, there was no doubt that the sudden change of tactics by Maxim was causing him all sorts of problems. He had weathered heavy punishment but by the end of the round Maxim seemed to have the measure of him.

Causing all the damage was Maxim's left uppercut. Knowing that he could not allow the American to get the punch off, Freddie used the sixth round to fight at long range, trying to create some distance. Although he sporadically drove at the body, even this was a high-risk tactic as Maxim was able to score with short right and lefts. Desperate as Freddie was to avoid the damaging uppercuts, one got through and drove his gum shield high into his mouth.

Dazed and confused, Freddie was in trouble and fighting on instinct. Seller failed to offer any advice other than to stay away from the punches, which were a red blur to Mills.

In the seventh, Freddie again went downstairs, beginning with a heavy left hand to the body of Maxim, who grimaced upon impact. But it was a mirage as the challenger was fully in control of the bout. When they got in at close quarters, Maxim would smash his deadly uppercut into his opponent's face.

A fraught Mills, looking for the one punch that would at least even the fight up, swung violently with his right hand and missed. This made him look clumsy and he was met by a huge shot from Maxim, further damaging his mouth and driving him to the ropes. Maxim was quickly on top of the hurt champion, raining blows on him. Freddie held his gloves about his head but was no longer throwing anything back.

The former milkman from Bournemouth was in deep trouble. During the break, Freddie ran his tongue over his gums to find that two of his teeth had been knocked out and another was hanging from the root. Freddie was forced to ask Seller to pull the other one out. He was breathing heavily, his head pounded and he was not sure where he was.

At the beginning of the eighth, Mills threw himself at Maxim but to no avail. The American had the number of the champion. The left uppercut that had been so effective throughout the bout was being thrown freely, inflicting even more damage.

Showing real heart, Freddie refused to stop swinging. His left hand found some success but his right let him down. Wild swings made him look cumbersome, giving the impression that Maxim was in control the longer the fight went on. Still, Freddie was terrier-like and followed up a good left with attempts at some work to the body.

The American challenger was just too fast and slick for Mills. After the fourth round, he had stopped clinching. Every attack from Mills was met with two-fisted aggression from Maxim, who was more clinical and placed his shots, looking to open up the Bournemouth man for the painful left hook.

At the end of the round Mills was tired, he was breathing heavily, his head was in a fog and he had run out of ideas. For every punch he threw, Maxim landed two or three in return, but there was no talk of stopping the bout. Ever since the first Lesnevich fight, there was a belief that Freddie could withstand punishment and still find a way back, but it was not to be on this occasion.

In the first few seconds of the ninth round, Maxim charged across the ring at Mills. At close quarters, fighters know when the strength is leaving their opponents. In each clinch Freddie was weakening. There was now less power in his punches than there had been in the earlier rounds.

The American sensed blood and went after the champion. Using combinations, Freddie only stalled his opponent's advance with a good left hook to the head. However, as he tried to move forward, Maxim then struck with a stinging and painful left jab to the face. Mills could only throw light jabs to Maxim's body, followed by wild swings that only connected with thin air.

The challenger almost seemed to be toying with Freddie. When the British champion attacked, Maxim either used his left jab or lateral movement, closing in with both hands. His speed was so fast it disorientated Mills, who once again was taking a lot of punishment.

As Freddie sat on his stool, it was as if he was resigned to the knowledge that it was only a matter of time before his legs gave way under a barrage of blows. A huge left hook at the beginning of the tenth was the last serious action of the fight as far as Freddie was concerned. Maxim responded with a left of his own that clearly hurt the Brit. This was followed by a torrent of punches, each thrown with real spite behind them.

In the greatest of ironies, Mills, who was renowned as a body puncher, was finally felled by a punch to the body after one minute 56 seconds of the round. Just as he began gasping for breath, a pulverising right to the jaw saw him crumble to the floor. It was a sad ending for the champion, who fell back against the ropes after being put on the floor on all fours. The referee began the count but he could have reached 100. There was no way Mills would have got back up. Freddie had no clear recollection of the previous two rounds and the last blow that sent him to the floor had caused him to black out.

As Freddie was counted out with his head resting against the bottom rope, the thumb of his glove was held against his nose and his eyes were closed in pain. The accuracy of the blows meted out by Maxim had twisted and distorted his features like a piece of clay. As the referee raised Maxim's hand in victory, three of Freddie's teeth fell out of his glove, having become embedded during the course of the fight.

In a daze, Freddie posed for press photographs with Maxim. All he could think of was rushing back to the dressing room to throw up again. Once there, the room began to fill up. Sitting with journalist Pete Wilson, Freddie almost wrote the obituary for his own career.

Explaining his inability to take a punch, Freddie told the reporter he had never really been the same fighter since the first Lesnevich fight. 'You see, Pete, when a boxer takes a caning like that, his fighting days are numbered.'

Just as Freddie was getting dressed, Joey Maxim continued the British tradition of the winner visiting the loser's dressing room. 'You're a nice fellow, knocking three of my teeth out!' said Freddie.

'And so are you,' responded Joey. 'You've cracked my front bridge work.'

'Well, well,' Freddie answered. 'It'll be a race to see who gets to the dentist first in the morning! Anyway, you know you get it free in this country, don't you?'

Both fighters laughed. Days later, Freddie would see Maxim off at Waterloo. As he boarded his train on the journey home to the States, he promised Freddie that if he could get in shape then he would happily give him a rematch, this time back home in New York.

Two years later, in 1952, Maxim would face Sugar Ray Robinson, who collapsed with heat exhaustion in the 14th round. Maxim would lose the championship to Archie Moore in December that year. Apart from winning an eight-round unanimous decision over a young Floyd Patterson, Maxim's career petered out. Losing his last six fights, he called it a day in 1958. In later life, he became a greeter for Las Vegas hotels and casinos before passing away in 2001 aged 79.

Despite promises of another bout, observers at ringside knew one thing was sure: Freddie Mills was finished as a boxer. There would be no more capacity arenas and no more big fights. He would have to find another way of making a living.

21

Doing the business

A PHONE call finally brought the curtain down on Freddie's boxing career. It was from a distraught Chrissie Mills to her father Ted Broadribb. 'There is no way Freddie is going to be fighting again. He's not got out of bed for three days, can hardly move and no one can understand a word he says. I want you to tell him it's over.'

Later that day, Broadribb went round to see Freddie at Joggi Villa and found him in a sorry state. Lying in bed, Freddie's face was grotesquely enlarged. At first, he did not recognise Broadribb when he walked into the darkened room.

Speaking softly, Broadribb told Freddie he didn't want to see him take any more punishment in the ring and therefore was unwilling to continue as his manager. Through his swollen mouth and broken teeth, Freddie rasped the word 'no'.

Once Freddie was up and about, he was confronted with a *News of the World* headline that read 'Why Freddie Mills will not be seen in a boxing ring again'. It was part of an exclusive interview with his manager, who told the paper that Freddie had been in one too many wars in the ring. Fearing for his health, he had advised him to retire and enjoy life.

As he read the epitaph on his career, Freddie's hands shook with rage. Ted Broadribb had got him into trouble with the taxman and was now telling the world he had retired. After making loud threats, Freddie finally calmed down when Chrissie told him it was her decision. He owed it to her and Don Jr not to have to live with the worry of him getting seriously hurt every time he fought.

Over the next few days, Freddie sank into a deep depression. At the age of 30, he was in no way a wealthy man and had been frightened by the demand from the taxman. For weeks before signing to fight Maxim, he had worried he was going to be destitute. He did want to go through that again.

Freddie thought to himself 'just two more'. A return with Joey Maxim, if successful, could secure a fight with the most famous boxer in the world, Sugar Ray Robinson. This would probably be one of the most lucrative bouts of all time. He could retire never having to worry about money ever again.

It was a pipe dream and Ted Broadribb told him so when he put the idea to his manager. If Broadribb would not manage him, then he would do it himself. So Freddie went off to Old Windmill Street and the offices of Jack Solomons to negotiate a rematch with Joey Maxim.

'Sorry, Freddie that newspaper story has ruined it. People think you are over the hill. I could not sell you in a fight with anyone, let alone Maxim,' Solomons told an emotional Mills.

Since the age of 14, boxing was all Freddie had known. He could never imagine life without it. Taking pity on the man who had been involved in some of the biggest fights ever staged in Britain, Solomons told him of two young prospects, featherweight Freddie King and welterweight Terry Ratcliffe.

Both were being trained by Nat Seller and were looking for a manager. Solomons told Freddie he could use his fame to help them climb the ladder. It was a great arrangement. Mills could keep his hand in boxing while Solomons would retain control of the pair.

As they shook hands on the deal, Solomons handed over a business card to Freddie. Written on it was the name of a theatrical agent the promoter advised was an old friend and who could help him cash in on his name.

It was not the first time Freddie had used his celebrity to make money. Upon his return from India in 1946, he became friendly with businessman George Ribey and builder Charles Luck. They had an idea for a business venture that intrigued him. Servicemen who had returned from the Far East after the war told their families of the exotic food they tasted there and wanted them to try it. Both Ribey and Luck were sure there was a market for Chinese cuisine.

Their plan was to open a Chinese restaurant. All Freddie had to do was invest £2,000 towards the £10,000 for the lease. Both Ribey and Luck would run the business while chef Andy Ho would manage it day to day. Freddie would lend his name to the restaurant, turn up on the odd occasion to regale some boxing stories, sign a few autographs and pose for pictures. Therefore, the Freddie Mills Chinese Restaurant opened at 143 Charing Cross Road later that year.

Cashing in on the new-found popularity of Chinese food, business boomed. At the same time, Freddie's media career was coming along nicely as well. Two months after he retired, he took part in the first outside boxing broadcast, providing commentary and expert analysis for the heavyweight bout between Dennis Powell and American Mel Brown.

By the mid-fifties Freddie was a presenter on the BBC's *Six-Five Special*, the first programme aimed at the teenage market. It was on this show that Freddie was to form a close bond with crooner, Michael Holliday, often socialising together. He also struck up a partnership with Dickie Henderson on his self-titled show, each week Freddie would play the stooge to the comedian.

Even though Freddie teased about a boxing comeback every so often, by 1957 he no longer needed the sport to provide income. His earnings from his restaurant and media career had been shrewdly invested in a series of flats and bedsits throughout London. According to his estate agent Bill Bavin, Freddie enjoyed an income of more than £3,000 a year from property alone.

Freddie's last link with the boxing world was broken when he sold the contracts of Freddie King and Terry Ratcliffe to his old trainer Nat Seller. Even that venture had not been unsuccessful, with Freddie taking both fighters from small shows in Bristol to the Empire Hall at Olympia.

Boxing lay in the past for Freddie. It was showbusiness that was now his consuming passion, even if it meant causing serious tension in his marriage. If things were going well in his career, the same could not be said of his home life.

Since his retirement from the ring, Chrissie had noticed a change in Freddie. He could be short-tempered with her and the children. As he spent more time with his new showbusiness friends, his mannerisms changed and he began addressing everyone as 'darling'. Girls swarmed around him at the restaurant and he seemed to revel in their company. Chrissie suspected it was only a matter of time before Freddie gave into temptation.

Even when Freddie was at home he was distant, going out at strange times but putting it down to business. One day, his secret was revealed. While collecting up some clothes to be cleaned, a letter fell out of one of Freddie's trouser pockets. It was from a woman declaring undying love, urging him to summon up the courage to leave his wife.

After a late night meet-and-greet with customers at the restaurant, Freddie returned to Joggi Villa to be confronted by a stoic Chrissie, who was waiting for him at the kitchen table. She had been there for hours rehearsing what she was going to say upon his return home.

'I want you to pack your things and leave,' she told Freddie. He looked at her quizzically. Throwing the love letter at him, Chrissie told him she knew all about his affair and wanted him to go to the woman.

Rather than deny the whole thing, Freddie sat opposite his wife and confessed everything. She was a chorus girl, who Freddie had met while being paid £150 a week on a variety tour with comedian Dickie Henderson.

Over an 18-month period, they had visited towns and villages all over country, taking Freddie away from his family for weeks at a time.

With little to do after the shows were over, Freddie had grown lonely and the woman had provided comfort. He had got in too deep. The affair had lasted for three years. He reached into his suit and pulled out a set of keys. 'Here's her flat keys, you take them. I only want you and the girls, mummy.'

'Why have you got her flat keys?' Chrissie asked. 'Are you paying to hole up your fancy piece?'

'I was only trying to help the poor girl out,' replied Freddie.

Chrissie was incredulous, screaming at him. She pounded Freddie with her fists. Soon, Freddie was in his car driving around the capital trying to think of somewhere to stay. For the next couple of nights, Freddie would regularly visit Joggi Villa hoping Chrissie would let him in.

Eventually, Chrissie opened the door. Freddie fell to his knees in tears. 'Please mummy, take me back. I miss you and the girls. I can't live without you. If I can't see my girls, then I may as well be dead.'

Trying to remain stoic, Chrissie told Freddie he had caused too much hurt to expect to walk straight back into their lives. If the truth be told, the girls had been asking why they had not seen or heard from their daddy for days.

Freddie pleaded with his wife to take him back until the early hours of the morning. Using every trick in the book to gain Chrissie's sympathy, Freddie argued it was unfair on the girls to have to live with the stigma of divorced parents. Neither could he could live with the public humiliation. In desperation, Freddie finally threatened to kill himself.

Relenting, Chrissie finally agreed that Freddie could move back into the family home under a number of conditions. 'I want you to ring that girl first thing in the morning and tell her it's all over and that you will no longer be paying her rent,' she demanded.

Freddie simply nodded his agreement. 'You can sleep in the spare room. I am only taking you back for one reason and one reason alone – for the sake of my girls. They love you and it would break their hearts if they knew what you were really like.'

Asking Chrissie to open her hands, Freddie placed a set of flat keys in her palms. 'This is her flat keys. Get rid of them. I do not want them anymore.' The following day, after Freddie had phoned the girl to tell her the relationship was over, Chrissie threw the keys out with the rubbish.

But Freddie had not ended the relationship at all. That night, when he told Chrissie he was going to the restaurant, he stopped off to see his girlfriend. Explaining the situation to her, they both simply resolved to be more careful in future.

Some days, Freddie wondered how long he could keep the charade going. He was adept at keeping secrets. Over the years, they would become deeper and more troublesome.

22

Holliday

IT was mid-morning on 29 October 1963 and Freddie turned on the radio at Joggi Villa. He could not believe what he heard. The crooner Michael Holliday, a huge star in the 1950s, had been found dead. Suicide was suspected. He was only 38 years old.

Ever since they met on the *Six-Five Special*, Holliday had become Freddie's closest friend. The night before, Michael had told Freddie he wanted to end it all. His wife had left him and he had been hit with a tax bill he had no means of paying off. Freddie had spent hours trying to talk him out of it.

Falling back in an armchair, Freddie sat still in shock. Michael had agreed to put any such thoughts out of his head when they parted company the night before. After all, tomorrow was a new day.

Running out to the garden he grabbed hold of Chrissie, crying into her shoulder. 'It's Mike, he's only gone and done it. I failed. What good am I if I cannot talk a man out of his taking his own life on my own doorstep?'

It had all been so different just six months earlier. Standing on a stage overlooking a crowded dance floor, Freddie introduced Michael as Britain's answer to Bing Crosby. It was the opening night of the *Freddie Mills Nite Spot* and, alongside Arthur Haynes and Alfred Marks, Michael was there to croon his biggest hit, 'The Story of My Life'. Freddie was in his element, with his showbusiness pals mixing with his mates from the boxing world.

'It's going well, mummy,' Freddie smiled, giving a thumbs-up to Chrissie.

Chrissie did not smile back. 'Have you seen who's over there?'

'No, who?'

'The Kray brothers. They say they are the head of everything rotten in London. Who invited them?'

'I did, they are friends of mine, lovely boys. Come on, I will introduce you.'

Freddie knew the brothers only on a social basis. They had invited him along to a few of their own club openings, enjoyed the odd meal at the restaurant and had asked him to get involved in a few charity boxing nights they had organised. He had always found them to be polite and courteous to anybody in their company.

Calling out to Ronnie and Reggie, Freddie pulled a reluctant Chrissie over to the table where the twins were sitting. A laughing Freddie asked Ronnie, 'Do you know what my missus just said? She said you and your brother are the head of everything rotten in London. Tell her it's just a rumour.'

Fixing both Freddie and Chrissie with a menacing stare, Ronnie Kray's eyes narrowed. 'I wouldn't believe the rumours,' he said coldly.

Freddie's face dropped before Ronnie burst out laughing. 'Don't worry, Fred. We wouldn't do anything to you. You're too much of a handful for even us two. Let's have a picture!'

As Freddie posed for a photograph with the two East End gangsters, he whispered to Chrissie, 'See, mummy, nothing to worry about.'

Behind his broad grin, Freddie was a man who had a lot to be worried about. He had not learned his lesson from his boxing career and the taxman was chasing him again, this time over his earnings from his showbusiness years.

In 1959, Andy Ho and Freddie had become the sole proprietors of the restaurant. Charles Luck died and George Ribey decided he wanted to sell. Squeezed by new competitors, the restaurant was no longer the novelty it had once been and was now haemorrhaging money.

Both Luck and Ribey's business acumen had been sorely missed. The small property empire Freddie had built up with the help of Bill Bavin had been largely liquidated to keep the restaurant afloat.

It had not gone unnoticed that he was helping himself to takings from the till. This happened so often that Andy Ho raised it with Ribey and Luck at board meetings. Freddie explained it away by saying he used the money to entertain important clients.

Apart from a few bit parts and an appearance on *This is Your Life*, media work had begun to dry up. With the restaurant his only means of income, he desperately needed a new idea to turn his fortunes around.

It came one night as Freddie was driving home from Soho. It was staring him right in the face. With the restaurant operating in the centre of London's thriving nightclub scene, it made perfect sense to open one of his own. With his showbusiness contacts, he was sure he could build a thriving establishment.

The restaurant closed for refurbishment on New Year's Day 1963, reopening as the Freddie Mills Nite Spot on 9 May. Every last penny was sunk into the club. All Freddie's existing rental properties were sold and a mortgage for £4,000 was taken out on his beloved Joggi Villa to meet the cost of renovations, which came to £12,000 – nearly £6,000 over budget.

Just as the former restaurant had struggled against competition, the nightclub, which was tucked away in a basement, faced the same problem. Soho was dominated by high-end clubs that were bigger and provided better facilities and food. Freddie and Andy were facing an uphill battle to make the club work.

Still, Freddie put all this aside in a last-gasp effort to talk his friend out of ending it all. 'You cannot take your life, it's not yours. Your mother gave you that life to do something with,' Freddie told Michael.

'I have nothing, no wife, no career. I am yesterday's man. Do you want to know the last time I had a hit? Three years ago. That's a lifetime in the pop world. The kids want the Beatles these days.'

Certainly, Michael was a troubled soul. Despite being one of the biggest stars of the day, he suffered from stage fright. His wife had left him because of his chronic womanising. Then there were the rumours.

According to comedian Bob Monkhouse, Michael would try anything sexually. Women or men, it did not really matter. He had a liking for pornography and took part in sex parties. It was said, with his active encouragement, Freddie employed prostitutes in his club as a way of earning some extra money.

It was not long before the gossip reached Fleet Street. In July, just two months after opening his new club, there was a knock on the door at Joggi Villa. It was Peter Forbes, a journalist who worked for the *Sunday People*. He wanted to speak with family favourite Freddie.

'We have reason to believe there is an active prostitute ring being run in your club,' said the journalist.

'Don't be stupid. We have a few girls as hostesses but they are not prostitutes,' replied Freddie.

'Really?' asked the journalist before relaying a story to an astonished Freddie of how an undercover journalist had answered an advertisement for a job as a hostess. Interviewed by a waiter called Smith, she was told she would not be paid but had to make do with tips from grateful patrons.

If she was nice to Mr Smith, he would ensure she sat with the best paying customers. If she went home with the client at the end of the night, she could expect to make £20.

Freddie shook his head. 'You're making it up.'

There was more, Forbes told him a couple of days later. Two undercover journalists picked up a few hostesses at the club and went back to a hotel with them. They had already forked out £19 for half a bottle of gin, two bottles of champagne, mineral water and a plate of sandwiches. They were asked for even more money for what the girls termed as 'extras'.

'You print any of this and I will sue,' Freddie threatened, fearing his reputation would be tarnished.

'I am afraid to tell you that a number of your hostesses have previous convictions for prostitution. Now, do you have any comment to make?'

When the *Sunday People* ran the story 'Sort out your club, Mr Mills,' there was very little Freddie could say in his defence, except to meekly claim that both he and Andy had no knowledge of a prostitute ring being operated there.

If the article had been devastating, it was nothing compared with the way he felt when he heard the news of Michael's death. For days afterwards, Freddie could not bring himself to go to the club. He very rarely left home, spending most days crying inconsolably. Little did he know there was even more trouble in store for him.

Whilst sitting at home a fortnight after Michael's death, Andy Ho rang Freddie to tell him that two customers were causing a row, refusing to pay their bar bill. When he got to the club, Freddie found two men in a heated argument with the doormen and Andy.

'What's going on, chaps? asked Freddie.

'You run nothing more than a clip joint, mate,' one of the men answered.

'Okay, okay, I am sure we can sort this out.'

They could not. Freddie and Andy were forced to sue through the civil courts. They both sat and listened to how the two men were enticed to the club by a young woman. Once inside, they were served soft drinks by another pretty young woman when they motioned to leave. They were charged £50 for being in the company of the woman. Even though the court found in Freddie's favour, the damage had been done.

Walking away from the court, Freddie was faced with the familiar barrage of questions from journalists waiting outside. He answered every one in his usual chirpy manner. The one question he could not answer, however, was the one he had asked himself over and over again. How much more could he take?

His best friend was dead, the club had caused nothing but trouble and now his reputation was being destroyed. Freddie had become a desperate man.

23

The plan

THE early-morning birds were singing as dawn broke over Joggi Villa. Freddie was sitting by the poolside having long given up trying to sleep. Taking a drag on a cigarette, he inhaled deeply, lost in thought. This week, which was the 17th anniversary of his victory over Gus Lesnevich, was shaping up to be one of the worst of his life.

Just as he was recovering from a bout of ill health, Don Jr confronted him about his low mood. It had been troubling Chrissie for weeks. She knew it was something more than the pneumonia he had been suffering from. After protesting that everything was fine and dandy, Freddie finally told Don Jr what was troubling him.

'Look, Don, the club has [had] a hard few weeks. I have had a bit of a cash flow problem. Everyone is feeling it at the moment. It will blow over. It always does,' said Freddie with a smile.

What he did not tell Don Jr about were the missed mortgage payments on Joggi Villa. In his desk, which he kept under lock and key at the club, were several unopened official letters. They were from his bank manager asking him to come in and see him as soon as possible to discuss his finances.

Had Freddie gone along to see his bank manager, it would have made for an uncomfortable conversation. With the club losing money hand over fist, all other potential income streams had dried up.

His showbusiness career was all but over. In February, he had lobbied his agent hard to persuade the BBC to include him on their panel of experts for the televised rematch between Muhammad Ali and Sonny Liston. The response was humiliating.

The BBC said no one could remember Freddie as a boxer any more. He had no credibility and to younger audiences he was nothing more than a figure of fun.

As a sweetener, Freddie's agent told him he might be able to get him a part in a pantomime at Christmas, probably as one of the dames. It was a lifetime away from what Freddie was used to but he desperately needed money.

In an effort to get back into boxing, Freddie even paid a visit to Jack Solomons. He hoped to do a deal where he could manage one of Jack's young prospects but British boxing was going through a lean spell. 'Everyone is struggling,' Solomons said. On this occasion, he could not help.

However, there was a glimmer of hope on the horizon. Solomons introduced him to a friend who was looking to set up in the new legalised bookmaking industry. The idea was to open up a series of betting shops across the country with the name Freddie Mills Racing emblazoned over the door.

Freddie would have the same deal he had with Luck and Ribey in the early days of the Chinese restaurant. Solomon's friend would run the business day to day. All Freddie had to do was appear at the grand opening and do a bit of publicity every now and again.

There was just one problem. Freddie did not have the money to invest. He was mortgaged up to his eyeballs. He needed to sell the club but had no takers. That was when he hit on an idea.

All over London, nightclubs were being mysteriously targeted, venues burned down, staff beaten up and windows smashed. It was an open secret that many of these clubs were paying money to all sorts of gangs. These incidents were seen as punishment, meted out to club owners for not paying for protection.

What if Freddie's club was torched? The Krays had been at the club on the opening night. It would not take much to create the impression that Ronnie and Reggie had ordered the club to be burnt down as retribution for Freddie refusing to be part of their extortion racket.

The more he thought about the idea, the more he liked it. As long as the police were satisfied the club had been burnt down in a criminal act, the insurance company would pay out. He would then be able to pay off all his debts, be free of the club and invest in the bookmakers. Things would be back to normal in no time.

The plan was a disaster. One night after the club closed and he was alone, Freddie set light to some match boxes stuffed in a settee. After locking up, he went back to Joggi Villa expecting to receive a phone call telling him the club was ablaze. It never came.

Unbeknown to Freddie, one of the doormen had returned to the club to collect something. He found the sofa a smouldering mess. The matches had failed to ignite. The one piece of furniture Freddie had chosen to burn was fire-proof.

When the police turned up a few hours later to investigate, Mills concocted a story that five gangster types had been in the club the night before, acted in a very strange manner then left without saying a word. He was sure they were responsible. The police officer did not buy it. Something suspicious was going on.

Just as the club was about to begin the cabaret the following night, police returned in large numbers. The club was being raided.

They found nothing except an illegal gambling machine. However, it meant another court appearance for Freddie and Andy Ho.

Sitting in the garden of Joggi Villa, long before the world awoke, Freddie knew the papers would be carrying the story about how fallen boxing champion Freddie Mills had allowed his club to be used for illegal gambling and been fined £68. It was the end of his dream of attaching his name to a string of successful betting shops.

Stubbing out his cigarette, Freddie rested his thumb and forefinger against the bridge of his nose. His head throbbed. Everything he touched seemed to go wrong. It was then he came up with a new scheme. This time, he was determined not to fail. Later that morning, Freddie resolved to put the plan in place.

The knock at the door just after 9am at Queenstown Road, Battersea, startled May Ronaldson. It was Freddie, an old friend. May's family ran a rifle range at Battersea fun fair. She had met Freddie through the boxing booths some 30 years earlier and had come to think of him as one of the family.

It was Freddie's second visit of the day. He had called around earlier but there had been no answer. He told May he was getting his car fixed and thought he would pop in for a cup of tea. Besides, he had a favour to ask her.

'I'll tell you what I've come for. Have you got an old gun I can have. It's only for a gag. I'm going to open a fete at Esher on Saturday.'

May replied, 'Why the devil do you want a gun, Freddie?'

'I am going to dress up as a cowboy. It's just a gag and I have to have a gun to have my picture taken. You can't be a cowboy without a gun.'

'Freddie, will you ever change? Always game for a laugh. You're in luck, I have one here. It doesn't work, though.'

'Sounds perfect. Don't worry, I am not planning on shooting anyone except myself!' joked Freddie.

'Well, I am not sure, Freddie. You know how clumsy you can be!' They both laughed.

In her amusement arcade, May used .22 automatic rifles. The gun May handed over to Freddie was four years old and faulty. Sometimes it would misfire. It was unreliable and May had been meaning to get it fixed but it was one of those jobs she had never got round to.

After half an hour, Freddie left May's house carrying the gun. He was then seen in a remote woodland. He got out of the car carrying the gun and prepared to test it by shooting it into a tree. It was then he realised he had no ammunition.

Freddie cursed his bad luck. He could not get anything right. He had to think of a way of getting hold of some bullets but he simply could not ask May for some. He had to come up with a better idea.

'Here you are, May. The fete's been cancelled. There's no need for the gun. Besides [these are] bloody dangerous things in the wrong hands!' a cheerful Freddie joked as he returned the weapon to his old friend.

On Friday, Freddie again returned to May's house. The fete was back on, he told her. He would need the gun after all. As May handed over the gun for the second time, out of the corner of his eye Freddie spotted some ammunition on the mantelpiece and saw an opportunity.

'You know what, May? I fancy a cup of tea. You wouldn't be a love and stick the kettle on, would you?' As May went into the kitchen to make the tea, Freddie took his chance. He quickly grabbed the bullets and put them into his jacket pocket. May did not notice they had gone. He now had a gun. All he had to do was make sure it fired properly.

Freddie never dressed up as a cowboy because there was never a fete in Esher. The gun was all part of the plan he had come up with to bring an end to his problems once and for all.

24

Wake me up

THE moment Freddie had been preparing for had finally arrived. Having spent the previous 24 hours agonising over whether or not he would carry out his plan, he was sitting in the back of his car in a darkened goods yard with May Ronaldson's rifle lying diagonally on his lap.

Just after 10.30pm on Saturday, 24 July 1965, Freddie arrived in Soho. He parked his silver Citroen in Goslett Yard, a mews just behind his nightclub. He said a cheery hello to the doormen and walked inside. Once there, Andy Ho pulled Freddie into the small office they shared and handed him a sheaf of bills.

There were final demands for electricity, gas and more letters from the bank, this time threatening to close down his overdraft facility unless he spoke to the manager. To top it all, business at the club had been so bad that week that Andy told Freddie they would struggle to pay the staff.

Once Andy left to return to the bar, Freddie screwed up the pieces of paper and angrily threw them in the bin. Furiously hitting the desk with his fists, Freddie finally snapped. He could not allow the world to see him as a failure. It was then he made up his mind. He was going to take action.

Once he had composed himself, Freddie entered the bar area, sat on one of the stools and ordered a large whiskey. As he sipped from the tumbler, he surveyed the room. It was Saturday night, the club should have been packed. Instead, there were six people there and two were putting on their coats, getting ready to leave before the cabaret began.

One of the hostesses yawned and looked at her watch while two of the barmen played cards. It was going to be a long night. Soon, the artist would be on, singing to an empty room.

There was no money to pay her. The petty cash tin that Freddie kept in his office was like the club's tills, empty. He reached into his pocket and pulled out a pound note and some spare change, not even enough to cover her expenses.

Knocking back what remained of the whiskey, Freddie told himself it was now or never. He proceeded to walk briskly out of the club. Just as he was leaving, he told doorman Bob Deacon that he had had one too many and was going to his car to try to sleep it off.

'Be a pal and wake me up in half an hour, Bob,' Freddie winked before walking off.

There had been tension in the Mills household earlier that day. Chrissie had asked Freddie for money to go shopping but he had finally confessed to appearing in court with Andy that week and the resulting fine had left him short.

Unsurprisingly, Chrissie hit the roof. She had never liked Andy Ho and was convinced he was ripping Freddie off. Just a few weeks earlier, she had accused Freddie's business partner of being a freeloader to his face. They were no longer on speaking terms. Freddie had paid the fine in full himself.

On and on, they argued until Chrissie could take no more. Helping herself to funds she kept in a tin in a side draw, for a rainy day, she took their two daughters down to the shops. Freddie watched as Chrissie drove off in her Mini, waving to his girls from the living room window. He felt an overwhelming impulse to go the boot of his car, get the gun and take it to the garage.

In the end, he just could not do it. He prided himself on being a loving family man and he hated the thought of Susan and Amanda having to live with the sight they would come home to upon their return. He would wait for the right time.

Instead, he went upstairs and lay on the bed fully clothed. Eventually, he fell into a fitful sleep. He was awoken by the sound of Chrissie and the girls returning from their shopping trip. The time away from the house had done nothing for his wife's mood.

While keeping up appearances in front of their young children, Chrissie could barely look at Freddie. The very few words she said to him were usually cutting remarks about Andy Ho and the club.

After eating a meal in silence, Freddie complained of a headache and went back to bed. While he was upstairs, Don Jr called round asking if he could borrow his mother's car for a few hours. Chrissie reluctantly agreed but warned him she wanted it back early so she could visit the club later that night.

Since the admission of his affair a few years earlier, Chrissie watched her husband like a hawk and made a point of being at the club most Saturdays in case he was tempted to stray again.

After an hour in bed, Freddie reappeared. His two girls were pestering their mother to allow them to stay up past their bedtime to watch The Beatles on the *Morecombe and Wise Show*. Chrissie and Freddie clashed after he overruled her and told the girls they could stay up late. At the end of the programme,

Freddie tucked the girls in bed, kissed them goodnight and went off to change.

As usual, Freddie looked immaculate, dressed in a pristine white shirt, slim tie and navy blue suit. 'Just off to the club, mummy,' Freddie announced as casually as if he was popping out for a loaf of bread. Chrissie did not take her eyes off the television and lit a cigarette.

Bob Deacon watched as Freddie whistled while he walked into Goslett Yard. Once safely out of sight, Freddie opened the boot of his car and took out the gun. He snapped it in half and inserted two of the cartridges he had stolen the day before into the magazine. He then opened the back door of the car and sat on the back seat. Freddie stared into space and contemplated what he was about to do.

A tap on the window momentarily startled Freddie. 'You all right, Freddie? Andy says the cabaret is about to start.' It was Bob Deacon.

'I feel like shit. If you don't see me in the next half hour, come and wake me up. Thanks Bob.'

Back at Joggi Villa, Chrissie fretted. Don Jr was late. The babysitter had already arrived, Chrissie was dressed and ready for the club. For over an hour, she paced around the house. She knew it was a mistake lending Don Jr the car. Her imagination ran away with her. Freddie could be doing anything.

The clock was ticking for Freddie. If he did not do it soon, Bob would return and he would have missed his chance. Pushing the muzzle of the gun in the gap between the passenger seat and the door, he made sure it made contact with the car's interior panel and pulled the trigger.

The gun made a muffled sound. Freddie pulled the weapon back and saw it had made a hole in the door. The gun was working. He wound down the car window to clear the gun smoke, waiting for two minutes to make sure nobody had been alerted by the sound of gunfire. When no one came, he got into position for the final part of his plan.

As Chrissie sat waiting for Don Jr to turn up, she began to fret about Freddie's latest court case. She laid all the blame at the door of Andy Ho. There had never been any trouble with the police until Andy came along. It was Freddie's good name being dragged through the mud, not his. She made her mind up. He had to go and she was going to tell him tonight, whether Freddie liked it or not.

Sitting in the back of his car, Freddie pressed the muzzle of May Ronaldson's gun firmly against his forehead. The butt of the rifle was held in place by his knees. This was the only way of saving his family from the shame and humiliation of bankruptcy. He felt he had no choice. Better to die like a man than go on living a lie. That's the way Freddie saw it.

Closing his eyes, Freddie slowly counted backwards from ten before gently and deliberately pushing his thumb down on the trigger. At the last moment, the old fairground rifle slipped slightly and the bullet penetrated the corner of his right eye before entering his brain. Freddie was dead within seconds.

The headlights lit up the living room of Joggi Villa. Don Jr, accompanied by his wife, had finally shown up. Having no time for excuses, Chrissie jumped in the car with her son and his wife and sped off towards the club. Minutes after she left, the house the phone rang. It was answered by the babysitter. On the other end, a very agitated man kept asking over and over again in broken English, 'Where's Chrissie? Freddie has been taken ill.'

There was no way of getting a message to Chrissie. Upon their arrival at the club half an hour later, the trio of Chrissie, Don Jr and his wife were met by Andy Ho, who having told them he could not wake Freddie directed them towards the darkness of Goslett Yard. Little could they have known the horror they were about to encounter there.

25

Fallen hero

SOMETHING serious had happened, Chrissie and Don Jr sensed it. Once inside Goslett Yard, the white mini screeched to a halt and Chrissie dashed out with her son following close behind. Bob Deacon and Henry Grant, who Chrissie recognised as one of the waiters, stood near the back of the silver Citroen with the door open, calling Freddie's name and gently slapping his face.

'He was all right when I last checked on him about an hour ago. I opened the door and gave him a quick push on the shoulder. He made a sound but I thought he was fast asleep. Henry has just come back and told me he couldn't wake him,' Deacon told an increasingly frantic Chrissie.

Pushing both men out of the way, Chrissie slid in the back seat and put her arm around her husband. 'Freddie, Freddie, it's Chrissie.' There was no response.

Freddie felt cold but initially Chrissie thought it was just the weather. It had been unseasonably cold for July and Freddie had taken to wearing a vest. She pulled her husband in close, feeling something warm against her chest. Looking down, she recoiled in horror. Her white blouse was covered in blood, as was Freddie's face.

It was then she felt the cold metal against her legs. At first she thought it was a starting handle for the car, but there was no mistaking. It was a gun, just the type Freddie would use at the fairground when he was trying to impress their daughters by winning a coconut.

Chrissie wanted to scream but the words would not come out. Instead, she whispered to Don Jr, 'He's only gone and shot himself.'

There was pandemonium. Andy Ho, who had run after the car into the yard, was in tears. 'Is Freddie okay?'

'He's in a bad way. Call an ambulance,' Don Jr shouted at Freddie's business partner.

Even though the club was practically empty, it did not take long for word to get around. The man after whom the place was named was sitting gravely ill in the back of his car outside. The doormen struggled to hold back the small crowd who had gathered in Goslett Yard upon hearing the news.

One of the barmen, Michael Chelliah, who was friendly with both Freddie and Don Jr, rushed up to the car in the vain hope he could do something to help. 'It's too late, Mike, he's shot himself,' Don Jr quietly told him.

'Oh no, where?'

'In the mouth, I think.'

'We should take a look. Here, use my cigarette lighter.'

The two men ignited the flame. Under its flickering light, Freddie looked as though he had a slight smile on his lips, as if he was enjoying a deep sleep. The only indication there had been any violence in the car was the bullet wound, which appeared to be between his eyes. Even with the makeshift light, it was too dark to determine the position of the gun.

'Yeah, he's shot himself and it looks like he used this to do it,' Don Jr confirmed to Chelliah, showing him the gun he had picked up from the car, which had been lying next to Freddie.

After being told by Chelliah to put the gun back, Don Jr placed the weapon next to Freddie in the position he thought he first found it.

Panic gripped Andy Ho. The ambulance was taking longer than expected and he waited outside the front of the club for it to arrive, getting more and more distressed. When the emergency service did show up, they had trouble understanding what he was saying. 'He behind the club. He not waking,' Ho shouted at the ambulance men in broken English before directing them to Goslett Yard.

When they finally got into the mews, two paramedics, Tom Spalding and Leslie Rowe, discovered Freddie in an upright position, his hands resting on his lap. Lying next to him was a rifle with the butt part on the floor and the trigger guard pointing towards the front.

Checking for signs of life, Leslie Rowe was sure he could feel Freddie's pulse beating as his wrists were still warm. Instructing Tom Spalding to open the rear side door, both men half-dragged Freddie out and together got him into the ambulance. Spalding returned to the car, opened the rear offside door and took possession of the rifle. He would later hand it over to the investigating police officers.

Upon seeing how badly hurt Freddie was, Chrissie collapsed on the floor. There was no way she could accompany her husband to the hospital. Don Jr told his wife to take his mother to a friend's house in Dulwich. There was no point waking the girls. It was better to let them sleep, so they could be told at a more appropriate time.

As the ambulance made its way to Middlesex Hospital, those who had been at the scene and witnessed Freddie's condition knew there was little hope he could survive. The doctor took one look at the gunshot wound and detecting no signs of life officially declared Freddie Mills dead at 2am on Sunday, 25 July. He was just 46 years of age.

The inevitable knock on the door came at Dulwich just over an hour later. It was a police officer, who had come to inform Chrissie Mills that her husband of nearly 17 years had succumbed to his injuries and passed away. It was agreed that Don Jr would go with the police to officially identify the body.

A post mortem was carried out later that morning. It concluded that Freddie had shot himself through the right eye. There were no other marks on his body to indicate foul play and the police who recovered two cartridges from the back of the car were satisfied that Freddie had committed suicide.

In absence of a suicide note, the police asked both Chrissie and Don Jr whether Freddie had suffered from any sort of depression or threatened suicide before. Both described him as happy go lucky. What you saw with Freddie was what you got. 'He was everyone's friend,' they told officers.

Had anything else been troubling him? Apart from the recent bout of pneumonia, nothing came to mind. The article in the *Sunday People* had upset him at the time but he had got over that, Chrissie said.

When posed with the same question, Don Jr believed there had been some money worries. The club was not doing as well as Freddie had hoped but he had told his stepson he was sure the summer tourist season would turn its fortunes around.

Later that day, Andy Ho sat down with police officers. He painted a different picture of Freddie. According to his business partner, Freddie was a worrier who was not cut out for the nightclub business. In the last few days, he had been distressed about the future of the club.

Police then established the owner of the gun. May Ronaldson was greatly distressed at Freddie's passing and told police of Freddie's numerous visits to her house in the week. She said she would never, ever have given him the rifle if she had had any inkling of what he was planning to do.

Just five days later, on Friday, 30 July 1965, Freddie was laid to rest at a church service at St Giles Church in Camberwell. It was a day when the worlds of boxing and showbusiness came together to remember Britain's first real sporting superstar.

In attendance was Jack Solomons, Ted Broadribb and Nat Seller, the men so closely associated with Freddie's career. They were joined by Henry Cooper, who had replaced Freddie as the country's favourite boxer, and the opponent who set Mills on the road to boxing stardom, Len Harvey, who had come along to say a final goodbye.

From the entertainment industry came actor and former boxer Norman Wisdom, singer Frankie Vaughan and stand-up comedian Tommy Trinder, who all sent floral tributes. *Carry On* star Sid James, Bob Monkhouse and his comedy partner Denis Goodwin, who later committed suicide himself, completed the familiar faces in the congregation. Almost anonymous at the back of the church was police officer Leonard 'Nipper' Read.

Entertainer Bruce Forsyth gave a eulogy, telling those assembled how much the showbusiness world had embraced Freddie and come to think of him as one of their own. Speaking to the *Bournemouth Echo*, Freddie's mother Lottie called him 'the best son a mother could possibly wish for'.

After the church service, Freddie was cremated at Golders Green crematorium before his ashes were laid to rest at Camberwell Cemetery. The gravestone displays an etching of Freddie in full fighting pose. It reads, in huge letters, 'Freddie Mills, father and son who was loved and adored'.

26

Rumours

ON 4 August 1968, there was a loud knock at the door at Joggi Villa. The call was not unexpected. Chrissie Mills had been up until the early hours of the morning making pages of notes she would hand over to her visitor, who arrived at the appointed time of 2pm.

The dapper man Chrissie greeted on her doorstep was Detective Superintendent Leonard 'Nipper' Read, who had made a name for himself by arresting Ronnie and Reggie Kray earlier in the year on suspicion of murder.

The arrest of the Krays was big news and rumours had reached Chrissie that the wall of silence they enjoyed throughout their criminal career was beginning to crumble. Those who had been too intimidated to tell the police of their activities were now willingly volunteering information.

Ever since the coroner had ruled Freddie's death as suicide, Chrissie had become more and more doubtful of the official verdict. To her, it was flawed. The coroner, Dr Gavin Thurston, had sat alone without a jury and there was also a dispute over the medical evidence. Both Chrissie and Don Jr questioned why the Home Office pathologist, Professor Keith Simpson, who conducted Freddie's post mortem, never thought it unusual that Freddie had shot himself through the right eye.

Even the doctor, David Wingate, who examined Freddie when he arrived at Middlesex Hospital just after the shooting, had not been called to give evidence. To Chrissie, it looked like a cover-up.

From the onset, she felt there was dirty work afoot. The more she thought about it, the more she thought the man she married, the father of her girls, would never kill himself. She remembered what he had said to Michael Holliday the night before he committed suicide. 'Life is there for the taking, go out and grab it with both hands.'

Even Freddie's old promoter Jack Solomons had warned her in the days after Freddie's death, 'If Freddie was standing here now and said "I have shot myself", I would never have believed him. Be careful, my girl, they are going to say it was a suicide.'

It had been a tough few years for Chrissie since Freddie's passing. For a man who was estimated to have earned £100,000 in his boxing career, Freddie only left an estate worth £3,767 19s 7d, which was reduced to £387 6s 5d after all the debts had been paid off. The club that had caused Freddie so much heartache in his final years closed its doors just two months after his funeral.

At the time of the closure, there was the very real prospect that Joggi Villa, the house Freddie so loved, would be repossessed. It was only a star-studded benefit night featuring some of Freddie's friends in the entertainment industry at the Prince of Wales Theatre in February 1966 that ensured Chrissie kept a roof above her and her daughters' heads.

When Nipper Read arrived at Joggi Villa that summer morning, Chrissie had been providing bed and breakfast for those who found themselves in need of somewhere to stay for the night. It provided a decent income and ensured she could keep up with the mortgage payments.

The senior police officer had come to meet Chrissie having received a letter from her asking him to re-investigate Freddie's case in the wake of the arrest of the Krays.

A boxing man to his fingertips, Read – a former fighter and official of the British Boxing Board of Control – was intrigued. Apart from wanting to build the strongest case possible to secure the conviction of Ronnie and Reggie, Read had also idolised Freddie, like so many of his generation.

Over tea and biscuits in the lounge of Joggi Villa, Read listened intently as Chrissie set out her theory of how Freddie had met his end in Goslett Yard three summers earlier. Just before Freddie's death, another small club owner, a former wrestler, who refused to pay protection money to associates of the Krays had been told 'that something big would happen up the west end to serve as a warning to him'. Two weeks later, Freddie was found dead.

To Chrissie, it all fitted. The missing money in his will had been given over as extortion money to the Krays. Knowing of the threat, he had armed himself with the old fairground rifle from May Ronaldson.

On the night he died, Freddie had met someone in Goslett Yard who had grabbed the rifle from him and shot him in the eye.

With Freddie out of the way, the Krays were then in a position to take over the club.

The reason they did not was because they were taken by surprise at the adverse reaction to Freddie's death and feared a public backlash.

As Chrissie talked, Read studiously took notes. 'I would love nothing more than to find Freddie's killer if I can, Mrs Mills,' said the Detective Superintendent.

'That is wonderful news. At least something is going to happen now at long last,' Chrissie said. After so many sleepless nights, she finally felt she would get the answers to all the questions Freddie's death had left behind.

It was not to be. Despite poring over every last document in Freddie's police file, he could find nothing. The pathologist's report was clear, the gun was too close to Freddie's skin for someone else to have inflicted the wound.

When Read asked his underworld contacts whether Freddie's death had served as a warning to others, he was told, 'If someone owes us money we break their legs, not kill someone else as a warning. Besides, if someone was going to bump him off they would use their own gun, something they could trust, not a rusty old rifle.'

Members of the Kray gang known as the firm, who were happy now Ronnie and Reggie were safely locked up, laughed off any suggestion Freddie was paying the brothers protection money. 'He was their idol. They loved being around the boxing community.

'If they did Freddie in, they would have been shunned and they would have hated that.'

Besides, those who accompanied the twins first to Freddie's restaurant and later to the club said the gangsters were insistent about paying their way and almost childlike in their adoration of the former champion.

The only significant new evidence Read had been able to glean from his sources was that Freddie was a gambler and a particularly long losing streak had added to his financial woes.

This, it was thought, was the reason he had helped himself to money from the club's takings.

When Read appeared at Joggi Villa to report his findings back to Chrissie, the result was disappointing. There was not a shred of evidence to link either Kray brother with the death of Freddie. After careful consideration based on the evidence, Read agreed with the coroner's official verdict. Freddie, close to bankruptcy, had taken his own life.

Up until her own passing in 1994, Chrissie would not accept the official verdict. When, in 1977, serious crime squad commander Wallace Virgo, who led the initial investigation into Freddie's death, was found guilty of corruption by taking bribes from the Soho sex industry, Chrissie felt he had played a part in covering up the Krays' role in Freddie's death. But she was clutching at straws. The allegations had no foundation.

From the moment word got around that Freddie had been found dead, the police received a mountain of anonymous mail from people all over the country claiming responsibility or having knowledge of Freddie's demise. Many of these contained inaccurate information and were quickly dismissed.

However, in 1980, Bournemouth Council, which was looking to erect a lasting memorial to their favourite son, received an unsigned letter of its own. It alleged Freddie was a serial killer who had murdered six prostitutes around the Hammersmith area in the 1960s then committed suicide as the net was closing in on him.

The council took the accusation seriously, with its public relations manager writing to the Chief Constable of the Metropolitan Police to ask him whether it was true Freddie was the serial killer known as Jack the Stripper. The name came about as each body had been stripped of its clothing.

A few weeks later, the Met wrote back telling the council Freddie was never a suspect in the case and they were satisfied with the original verdict of suicide.

This was not the first time questions had been asked about Freddie's potential involvement in the case. Nipper Read had asked the police officer in charge, John Du Rose, who told him Freddie had nothing to do with it. Two of the bodies had been stored in an industrial estate and the man they were interested in was a security guard who worked there.

The only evidence presented was circumstantial. The police said the culprit had died before he could be arrested, which is why the murders came to an end in early 1965. Freddie was found dead in July of that year. Even though he had never been arrested on suspicion of the murders, this did not stop people putting two and two together and coming up with five.

There was to be more anguish for the Mills family in the coming years. Any piece of gossip was reported as fact. The rumours surrounding Freddie's death took on a life of their own.

Chrissie Mills would live to see her husband accused by the *News of the World* of being secretly gay, having allegedly had a relationship with Ronnie Kray then killed himself before he was due to appear at Westminster Magistrates' Court charged with procuring young men for sex.

Claims of Freddie being gay were nothing new. For years, it was claimed he enjoyed relationships with Don McCorkindale and Michael Holliday. However, there is no evidence to suggest any of these allegations by the newspaper were true. There was no scheduled court appearance and only the word of others to suggest gay liaisons. The stories were always accredited to an underworld source, who never gave their name.

Many of these theories were given further credence in the eyes of the public with the appearance of books such as *Who Killed Freddie Mills?* by journalist Tony Van Der Burgh. The author claimed that Chinese gangs wanting to take over Freddie's nightclub so they could deal drugs and indulge in other criminal activity took out a contract on his life. But by the time Freddie died, if the Chinese or anyone else had wanted the club they could have had it. It was worthless.

Freddie's close friend Peter McInnes, in his book *Freddie Mills, My Friend,* was firmly of the opinion that Freddie had been murdered by the Krays. He even went as far as to his claim that his own life was put in danger following an angry confrontation with Charlie Kray, the twins' older brother, in a pub in Bournemouth.

The only theory worth exploring further is that Freddie, suffering from the effects of successive concussive blows, was in the late stages of a condition known as chronic traumatic encephalopathy (CTE), a degenerative condition caused by repeated blows to the head. It can lead to dementia and thoughts of suicide.

The symptoms include the dizziness and blinding headaches that plagued Freddie in later life.

However, without a full physical examination of Freddie's brain, it is impossible to assert whether he suffered from the condition. Therefore, like all other rumoured causes of his death, it is just speculation.

Either way, it does not matter now. Freddie's daughter Susan said, 'It is irrelevant now whether it was suicide or he was killed, as some people think. Whatever happened, it will never bring him back. I am so happy I was able to have that sort of person as a father.'

For many fans, their most abiding memory of Freddie will be of the night he conquered the world. As he stood in the ring at White City, eyes ablaze, arms aloft, for a brief moment he encapsulated the hopes of post-war Britain. With the world championship belt around his waist, and the rapturous crowd singing his name, he ascended to the level of an icon. Despite what happened afterwards, on that night Freddie Mills was glorious.